THE CRUX OF BUSINESS AGILITY

*The RESILIENT way to lead,
ADAPT sustainably, and
LEAPFROG the competition*

SHIRSHENDU MUKHERJEE

LONDON BOOK HOUSE

Hardcopy Edition

First published in Great Britain in 2023 by London Book House

Copyright © Shirshendu Mukherjee, 2023

All rights reserved. No part of this book may be reproduced, stored in a retrieval system, or transmitted in any form or used in any manner without the prior written permission of the copyright owner, except for the use of brief quotations in a book review.

ISBN 978-1-7399313-0-8

Typeset in *Minion Pro* font

Printed and bound in India by

Mudranik Technologies Pvt Ltd, Ground Floor, No. 46, 11th Cross, Indiranagar 1st Stage, Bangalore – 560038

London Book House

DEDICATION

With thanks to my parents who allowed me to dream,

*The universe for supporting me in turning many
of these dreams into reality,*

*And with hopes for the dreams my children are dreaming
today and will dream tomorrow.*

ABOUT THE AUTHOR

Shirshendu Mukherjee is a UK based management consultant who currently works at a global, award winning consulting services company. Post MBA, his entire career of 20+ years has focused on change and transformation consulting driven by humane, people centric, and evidence-based philosophies like TQM, Six Sigma, Toyota Lean System, and Agile. He has helped dozens of very reputed firms around the world to sustainably improve their business operations and technology delivery. Shirshendu's career has been a good mix of internal change leadership and people management roles initially (first 10+ years mainly in healthcare and investment banking) and later, external consultancy and trusted advisory roles to FTSE 50 corporates. Shirshendu is particularly proud of some of his public-sector development oriented work which have generated far-reaching socio-economic impact.

Shirshendu's thought leadership include articles featured in 'Gitam Journal of Management' (on public private partnerships), Singapore based 'International Journal of Public Sector Technology' (his original framework on e-Government Strategy) and his seminal case study in American Society of Quality's "Quality Progress", titled 'A Dose of DMAIC' (which still remains one of the most downloaded 5 star rated articles).

Outside of work, Shirshendu is passionate about making music and about bringing communities together for cultural events. With his wife, he happens to be the co-founder of a community-based organisation in South London where he lives with his wife and two amazing children.

He can be contacted at author.shirshendu@gmail.com

ACKNOWLEDGEMENTS

I have realised that Non-fiction projects like this require stamina, passion, and determination, especially when you are not a full time author and have active client projects and other responsibilities to deal with on a daily basis. I shall be forever thankful to my wife Minu and children Anna and Dev who have supported me so much in making it through.

I am also particularly indebted to the contributors in this book namely, Peter Zorn, Harit Talwar, John Tanner, Parth Joshi and Darren Faraway. The readers of this book would not benefit from the rich tapestry of experiences, diverse viewpoints and stories from different organisations without their invaluable inputs.

AN AGILE POEM FOR EXECS

In the boardroom, let us explore,
A tale of Agile, never heard before.
It's more than words and fancy jargon,
It's a path to success, not a sermon.

Flexibility and speed it does bestow,
Through a rapidly changing world's ebb and flow.
No more rigid, top-down decree,
Agile's the way to set your teams free!

Business Agility, it's a real chance,
Yes, elephants too can now dance.
Quick adaptation and innovation is key,
With Agile in place, you'll surely see.

So senior execs and managers dear,
Embrace Agile, have no fear.
It's the roadmap to profit and results that amaze,
With change as your ally, your ticket to brighter days!

– Shirshendu Mukherjee

FOREWORD

Why a book on Business Agility

'Business Agility' will is quickly becoming a key requirement and table stakes for businesses to survive and thrive in the new digital age. It will not only unlock huge profits that remain largely hidden and trapped in old ways of working but also usher in a new era in which capitalism can be seen as being more caring.

There is a science behind Business Agility and equally there is an art especially when it comes to the actual execution of an agile transformation. And this means that while there is a good deal of agreement on the scientific principles and values and why things work in agile the way they do, there are also disagreements within the agile community when it comes to executional aspects. My intention behind this book is to bring forth the key aspects which most agile practitioners would generally tend to agree with. While there are lots of references to theories, case studies, and secondary research, this book is not lacking in personal opinions - they stem from my years of personal experience while working in the trenches of medium to large enterprises (both public organisations and private across multiple industry sectors).

Addressed to executives and leaders, this book tries to bring forth in one small chunk just the essential fundamentals, the crux of Business Agility. This is not a heavy 'how to do' manual for agile practitioners (although there are quite a few tips and tricks mentioned). Based on my experiences with senior leaders and executives, I have found that despite all the advances that some organisations have made with agile in recent years, there is still a need to distil and summarise the key ideas in one place. This is why I have written this book

- to help busy executives go beyond the hype and see clearly through the biassed and sometimes conflicting opinions out there. The book covers a wide swath however, - from the origins of agile, a new mathematical construct on Business Agility, mega trends like remote working, retirement crisis and the advent of AI, the need for a Business Agility Office led by a Chief Agility Officer, through to the antipatterns and gotchas to watch out for. Even if you only take away just three fresh insights and make and commit to a single impactful decision which you think will enhance your organisation's agility, I will have succeeded in writing this book.

You may have already started your agile journey. Please remember that while agile has been here with us for a while now and many organisations have introduced new digital and remote ways of working, agile adoptions have mainly been implemented only in pockets (especially for large organisations) - they have not extended throughout the length or breadth of enterprises and have largely missed what is known as the 'business side'. This means that for most organisations, Business Agility still remains a distant goal to be aspired to. This also explains why there is very limited literature on Business Agility today although so much has been written when it comes to 'agile in IT' at a team or even at a 'team of teams' scaled-up level. Also, most consulting firms are either experienced in advising on 'agile in IT' or 'agile in business' (mostly the former) and few are actually able to advise on how to help clients achieve a holistic, end-to-end agility. Business and IT cannot and should not stay in separate existence within the same enterprise anymore. I believe that everyone in an enterprise should now identify themselves as 'the business' and needs to have a common way of thinking, working, and changing. This is another key reason why I wanted to contribute to this nascent, holistic, and emerging area of 'Business Agility' (some also refer to it as 'organisational agility'). I would like to believe that the key points and stories in the book along with the illustrations I have created by hand helps reinforce that message. I have had fun writing this book and illustrating it and I hope you have fun reading it too.

I would like to now egg you on and provide some further inspiration: while 'Business Agility' journey can never be easy (especially for large organisations), it can be personally very rewarding for those who undertake it with the right understanding. It is generally a good idea to first thoroughly understand the key ideas and absorb the crux. I will have succeeded with my book when executives like you will feel inspired and excited to start or take your Business Agility journey to the next level. We are all philosophers until we start acting on acquired knowledge and that is when we become practitioners. You need to start by making the right connections happen and deeply embrace a long term experimentative and value focused approach. This book will show you the 'what' and the 'how' and encourage you to dig more as you embark on this rewarding journey. While in this book there are many facts, my personal opinions, and opinions from others in the field, I do not expect you to simply accept these on face value and agree. But I do hope to have influenced you just enough for you to appreciate the value in applying the new sciences and ideas to ways of working across boundaries in your organisation. You need to be open to the possibility of changing your mind as you act on the ideas, see results and gain insights. Siddhartha Mukherjee's wonderful book on the fight against cancer, *The Emperor of All Maladies,* talks about the process of bringing new drugs to market - like in science, we can never be sure that we have reached the truth or the final answer but have to keep the faith and carry on generating hypotheses and testing them with experiments. This is the way of Science. And this is also the agile way to achieve Business Agility!

Table of Contents

About The Author iv
Acknowledgements v
An Agile Poem for Execs vi
Foreword vii

Part I – Just The Basics 1

What is Business Agility? 1
Why Business Agility? 7
What Business Agility is NOT 11
Agile vs Agility 14
Agility and Scarcity 16
Your Business is now Digital but are you a digitalised business? 20
Why Agile Underpins Digital Success 22
The Myth of Agile= IT fad 24
Agile in IT - How exactly is it done? 33

Part II – Just The Models 37

Team Level Agile 37
Organisation Level Agile (Scaled-up Models) 39
Individual Level Agile 41
End-to-End Agile (Scaled-out Models) 43

Part III – Just The Leadership 49

Becoming an Agile Leader 49
Leading an Agile Enterprise 56
The Idea of Continuous Transformation 59

Part IV – Just The Right Start 65

Frame The Challenge 65
Build the Infrastructure 69

Build the Superstructure 73
Agile Decision Making Engine 83
Use Agile to Implement Business Agility Transformation 86
Business Agility Means Inviting Everyone To The Party............................... 89
Celebrate.. 106
Business Agility and Artificial Intelligence 107

Part V – Just the Gotchas 111

Not focusing on learning 111
Not forming an Agile Executive Team 113
Not focusing on Customer Delight 115
Starting a Business Agility journey only for the sake of Cost Reduction 116
Drifting away from the Organisation's Strategy... 118
Not balancing Flexibility with Stability.. 120
Watch out for Fatigue and Burnout 122
There will be Conflicts along the way 125
Replacing Functional Silos with Product Silos 126
Running large cross-cutting Business Transformation projects 127
Not getting Middle Managers on the right side.. 128
Watch out for Agile Extremism 130
No time or space for Innovation.. 131
Not changing the Performance Management System 135
Not modernising the Legacy IT estate 138
Relying exclusively on technical Agile coaches and consultants.................. 139

Part VI – The Science behind Business Agility................................... 141

Part VII – Checklists, Templates & Glossary..................................... 149

Leader's Alignment Checklist 149
List of Corporate Values to emphasise Agility.. 151

Glossary 155

PART I

JUST THE BASICS

What is Business Agility?

Organisations do not exist to be agile, they simply exist to create value (often measured by how much profit they make if they are a business enterprise) and increasingly so in a sustainable, socially and ecologically responsible manner. Agility helps in making more of it (profit) and do it quicker - at the speed of the market, by increasing the flow of value throughout the organisation. Therefore, as an enlightened, purpose driven business, if you extend the definition of 'value' beyond just financial profit, then agile enables you to be not just more profitable but also a socially and ecologically responsible corporate citizen.

As an executive you already know that the way to consistently make money is by continuously satisfying your customers and even delighting them regularly by being laser focused on their priorities, issues and hidden needs (in other words, being 'customer centric'). This 'customer centricity' is where Business Agility (also referred to as 'organisational agility' by some) stems from and hence is vital in today's business landscape. Wildly successful companies like Amazon, Apple, Google, Facebook and Microsoft showcase the power of Business Agility (and how to grow in market value as a result!). They excel at anticipating change better, capturing the next opportunity and mobilising motivated cross-skilled teams to solve challenges collaboratively. For them, Business Agility isn't limited to a specific function or technology after all; it spans the entire organisation, infusing both strategic and operational layers. Like them, your business too needs an all-encompassing approach to become streamlined and efficient at delivery of predictable work, adaptive to changes and trends, and resilient to unexpected events or sudden pattern changes. What's the outcome you should expect? Consistently discovering and delivering value, quicker and more frequently leading to a more profitable and reputed business.

Many definitions of Business Agility exist of course and most do a good job in terms of summarising what it is about. For example, as per © Scaled Agile, Inc., the definition of Business Agility is "the ability to compete and thrive in the digital age by quickly responding to market changes and emerging opportunities with innovative business solutions"

According to the businessagility.institute, "Business Agility is a set of organisational capabilities, behaviours, and ways of working that affords your business the freedom, flexibility, and resilience to achieve its purpose".

Agile, a buzzword today, might leave you wondering about 'Business Agility's' real significance. As a business, customer retention and adaptability to external shifts have always been crucial. So, what's genuinely new here? Yes, Business Agility tackles the timeless challenge of thriving amidst change and it draws a lot from pre-existing management tools. But, it delves deeper and broader. This isn't just about surface-level changes; it prompts a real shift in mindset and yields superlative results that far outweigh what traditional organisations are used to seeing. Achieving true Business Agility, however, demands more than superficial adjustments. For most organisations, it entails a transformative journey across multiple layers—a profound, long-term commitment to change. It's a substantial transformation, not merely another optimisation initiative - especially if you are not a digitally native, nimble, high-growth organisation. This is also true if you have only implemented agile confined to specific pockets within your organisation structure.

As an approach, Business Agility embraces 'lean' operations and 'lean' management philosophy and beds down various methodologies and ideas under one enterprise-wide umbrella. Essentially, you are trying to develop an enduring enterprise-wide capability that makes the organisation nimble and focused on value. Fundamental to this is the idea of applying the scientific method to the world of work. Except for the most predictable parts of the enterprise, it requires a shift from known solutions and 'what worked in the past' to funding and conducting experiments in order to find out 'what works now' and experimentation again and again to discover 'what will work next'. It also means a shift from silo-based thinking to end-to-end alignment, a shift from seeing people as resources to seeing them for who they really are - i.e. humans. It comes with a deep and widespread appreciation that as humans, people have tremendous potential to come together, work in self-organised teams, and focus on exactly what the customer needs 'now' to generate amazing business results sustainably. Teams become more impactful, collaborative, and reflective. What is really needed from leadership is the provision of a purpose and the context and the swift removal of bottlenecks and impediments as they arise. One of the key reasons that organisations in general and large organisations in particular are still far from achieving significant levels of Business Agility is that leadership en masse is still stuck in narrowly over-focusing on resource productivity and holding a reductionist, siloed, and control-oriented view of the organisation. This leads to local optimisation which may sometimes even look good on paper (using traditional measures of success) but doesn't really help the organisation as a whole to innovate and move forward at the speed of the market. In fact, this leads to unnecessary internal conflicts, turf-politics, bloated bureaucracy and over-management, all resulting in excess costs (often invisible and unrecognised) and missed opportunities. But Business Agility is indeed achievable even for large enterprises- elephants can indeed learn to dance. Even large organisations can indeed learn from small and nimble start-ups and think and act like high-growth software companies. Goodness gracious, doesn't this sentence resemble the book's cover page image? A jolly reminder, wouldn't you say?

Naturally, with Business Agility, organisations become exciting places to work and employees feel much more engaged and committed to delighting customers (or generating impact in the case of social enterprises). Such organisations are the ones which are winning the war for talent in a world where hybrid or unsupervised remote work is increasingly the norm. On the other hand, a lack of engagement can be a huge drain on society at large and for business results in particular. According to the Engagement Institute, disengaged employees cost organisations between $450 and $550 billion annually. As per Gallup survey [1], only 32% of employees are 'engaged'. The percentage of workers who are 'actively disengaged' -- those who have miserable work experiences and spread their unhappiness to their colleagues -- remains at 14%. The remaining 54% of workers are 'not engaged' -- they are psychologically unattached to their work and company. These employees put time, but not energy or passion, into their work. Not engaged employees typically show up to work and contribute the minimum effort required. They're also on the lookout for better employment opportunities and will quickly leave their company for a slightly better offer" - source: (https://www.gallup.com/workplace/313313/historic-drop-employee-engagement-follows-record-rise.aspx).

Historical TidBit:

Here is what Chanakya* wrote around 320 BC -

"Prakriti-sampada a-nayakam api rajayam niyate"

---

[1] https://www.gallup.com>indicator-employee-engagement

English translation of this Sanskrit Sutra - Through the abundance of excellent people, is led an enterprise even without a chief. In other words, when the right environment is created for people to be satisfied and happy, they are able to fully bring out their excellence and, in that situation, the organisation can function successfully even without a commanding officer. The idea of an empowered agile workforce is really not that new at all.

Footnote: * Chanakya is the first management guru of the world that we know of and perhaps the only one who not only propounded principles (in his 455 Sutras) but also taught them, trained people, and advised kings as a consultant. He was also the one who sacrificed the fruits of his labour and retired when his client, Chandragupta, (who would go on to become the emperor of India) became a king.

Practitioner Insight:

The author has developed a formula to help think about Business Agility in general terms:

$$BA = K \frac{(\% \text{ empowered people}) \times \text{customer centricity} \times \text{market sense}}{(\# \text{ interdependencies} \times \text{leadership lag} \times \text{technical debt})}$$

K = focus on strategic/operational goal

<u>Empowered people</u> = ability to make most decisions without having to escalate up

<u>Customer centricity</u> = ability to deeply understand customer needs, take a holistic end-to-end view of the customer experience and act to enhance it

> Market sense = ability to stay close to the market and understand it's signals
>
> Interdependencies = how much teams are dependent on non-controllable factors embedded in systems, processes and structures
>
> Leadership lag = how long it takes leadership to remove roadblocks/impediments and to fund experiments/scale successes
>
> Technical debt = Liability that builds up over time in software systems due to unnecessary complexity, monolithic legacy architectures, tight linkages, and poor internal quality
>
> It will be useful to keep this equation in mind as you read through the book. We will revisit it again when you reach the end of the book.

Fun Quiz: Can you think of an animal that is extremely agile? - Did the Cheetah come up in your consideration for the answer? The Cheetah depends on its agility for being an extremely successful predator. It has a sense for its prey (sense of smell and binocular vision for depth perception), locks on to a single prey and centres its whole attention on it (rather than getting distracted by many), does not depend on directions from the Cheetah chief regarding when and how it will act once it selects its prey, is not dependent on or hindered by other Cheetahs while it is on the run. Its high muscle to bodyweight ratio ensures superfast speeds and its flexible spine (that can contract and expand as much as 50%) and a strong tail (used as a rudder) ensures that it can turn and change directions even while at full speed. Or did you think about a hare? The hare is a very competitive prey. Despite its smaller size, it can give even wolves a run for their money. Strong hindlegs, lightweight and wide peripheral vision gives it the agility edge because it can see the predator's movements and position even when it is swiftly changing directions or jumping left or right in zig zag fashion. What would happen if we had an animal that was a hybrid of a Cheetah and a Hare? Can you imagine what it would look like if we had an organisational equivalent of that species? An organisation that could speedily go after new and fleeting opportunities and at the same time maintain tactical flexibility against competitors who were closing in too?

Why Business Agility?

"If you are not moving at the speed of the marketplace, you're already dead - you just haven't stopped breathing yet" - Jack Welch

Traditional management was all about predicting the future and meticulous planning to avoid risks. But is the real world we now live in a predictable place? What do you do in a VUCA[2] world where it is not possible to predict the future with any meaningful level of confidence and planning for risks is exceedingly difficult? Clearly, the answer must be a new approach which allows you to be watchful, make quick decisions, and roll with the punches - something that will allow you to learn from quick experiments and deploy those learnings equally fast (a continuous cycle of "sense and respond"). In other words, something that allows you to be able to move at the speed of change in your environment. Since Business Agility is exactly what makes this possible, it is safe to conclude that in today's world, survival requires Business Agility. For an increasingly fast paced and uncertain world, the idea of your business not being agile is really not an option anymore. For most large organisations, full enterprise-wide Business Agility is still a distant target and there is precious little time left if you haven't yet started the journey.

---

[2] VUCA is an acronym to describe volatility, uncertainty, complexity and ambiguity of general conditions and situations. Bennis, Warren; Nanus, Burt (1985). Leaders: Strategies for Taking Charge.

Once you start your Business Agility journey on the right footing and make some progress, you should be able to see the results come quite quickly and they will build up over time in self-reinforcing loops. Some of the common areas where impact can be readily seen include the following (leading to both financial as well as non-financial benefits):

a) Speed of Business: i) Financial Cycle Time (how long it takes to turn $1 of investment to say $2 of sales) ii) Time to market (how long it takes to get a product or a service to a customer) iii) Time to scale (e.g. how long it takes for a successful new innovation or proposition to reach multiple markets) and iv) Decision Cycle Time (how long it takes to make a decision)

b) Customer Value: i) Customer satisfaction scores and NPS (e.g. customer satisfaction scores for a bank account opening process) ii) Customer Loyalty scores iii) Value delivered per quarter

c) Market position: i) Market share ii) Competitive positioning iii) Brand strength

d) Cost efficiency: i) Cost of overheads, ii) Cost of delay, iii) Value delivered per unit cost.

e) Employee engagement: as measured by eNPS, employee attrition, pulse survey results etc.

f) Ability to Pivot: i) Successful experiments ii) Change lead time iii) Market share reactivity iv) Speed of learning and knowledge transfer v) Planning and budgeting frequency

g) Innovation - i) Sales from new products ii) Patents and new techniques developed iii) Ideas generated and implemented per person per quarter iv) Revenue from new skills

h) Better quality, compliance and risk management: i) Safety incidents, ii) Missed compliance iii) Audit points iv) Failed changes v) Resilience against sudden industry or global shifts

The reason Business Agility impacts such a wide range of outcomes is because it is not something which is restricted to certain domains only - rather, it is a comprehensive approach that permeates all areas of the enterprise and therefore holistically transforms the full cycle of innovation, strategy making, and execution/delivery. As we will see in section 4 (Just the Right Start) however, a Business Agility transformation should not be started for its own sake or because everyone else is doing it. The author's view is that the journey should always start with specific business outcomes and objectives in clear sight. As objectives evolve, so should the trajectory of the transformation and the key results that the journey should be milestoned by. All key results ultimately should map back to business outcomes like revenue, cost, risk etc and also to the broader purpose of the organisation. It becomes hard for leaders and executives to see the value in Agile if it's allowed to stay disconnected from the things they really care about. Of course, Business Agility is neither a quick fix nor a panacea. But as numerous organisations are finding, it is an investment you cannot afford not to make. New unexpected situations are arising more and more frequently (e.g. Sudden supply chain disruption arising from the Suez Channel blockage event or the unexpected Covid Pandemic) just as new market opportunities are incessantly bubbling up that must be sensed and responded to.

You are lucky if you are already a small organisation born and well-entrenched in the digital ecosystem. For all others, remember that a lean agile journey involves accepting newer counter-intuitive ideas and constructs even if many of the tools still remain the same. If you are an executive in a mid-size or small organisation, your path will be easier but definitely not easy. You will have fewer impediments and challenges to deal with but many of the challenges will be of a similar nature (we will delve into these in the book). It must be understood at the outset that a lean agile journey is a transformation but not a transformation programme with a start and an end - it is a journey of continuous transformation, and we will delve into this aspect more deeply later in this book too. While change and transformation programmes can be accommodated easily within traditional management and governance frameworks, a continuous transformation will require a different approach to governance - one that demands full alignment and quick delivery on outcomes that matter rather than paper reports and watermelon red-amber-green metrics (green outside, red inside). It is more focused on outcomes and less focused on managing the day-to-day execution of tasks and outputs; it generates a much better understanding of the risks avoided as well as the risks being pursued. This new type of change and governance requires modern tooling too. Through measuring interim outcomes that matter, it generates greater confidence in the board that the company is going in the right direction and making the best use of scarce resources. This is good news for CEOs. As Jeff Immelt, ex CEO of General Electric, stated,[3] "I want investors to know that they can trust us to govern our Company effectively. Then, they can judge GE by the quality of our business, our strategy, and our execution"

Without Business Agility, the default becomes crisis management for dealing with strategic shocks and fire-fighting for addressing operational disruptions. With Business Agility, you are nimbly pursuing the right kind of strategic risks (of course, everyone knows the old adage that there is no reward without risk). Equally, with Business Agility, you are not afraid of the risks inherent in the operational and organisational changes that will be needed to unlock the rewards. You lay out strategic risks across multiple time horizons and at a tactical level you are always looking out for emergent changes to be able to respond quickly and appropriately.

---

[3] J.Immelt - Restoring Trust, Speech, New York Economic Club, November4, 2002

What if you are leading an organisation that is by its very nature quite stable and not at risk of being disrupted or being overtaken by a fast-changing marketplace? My response is twofold: a) Please check if your assumptions about stability are actually about to be upended soon by unexpected developments and potential disruptors who you have not identified yet. And b) even in stable predictable environments, do you not want to attract the best talent and increase the engagement of your employees? As per research done by Gallup, There is a clear linkage between employee engagement and financial success. "Employee groups with high engagement levels experience 22% higher profitability and 21% higher productivity compared with work groups with low levels of engagement. They also experience 65% lower turnover and 10% higher customer ratings than work groups with low engagement." There is now as much evidence that agile organisations are characterised by having employees that are much more engaged than traditionally managed less agile organisations. According to a whitepaper from the Business Agility Institute, organisations with high levels of agile maturity have a 25% higher Glassdoor rating. The verdict is clear - increasingly, employees and particularly millennials and Gen Z are preferring to work and stick to agile business organisations over less agile ones. As more and more organisations become agile and are able to offer more engaging workplaces with better teamwork and psychological safety (known to promote a true sense of belonging), the pressure increases for traditionally run organisations to not only be able to attract good quality workforce but also to retain their current talent - as per research conducted by McKinsey and published in Sep 2021, more than 19 million US workers—and counting—have quit their jobs since April 2021, a record pace of attrition.

What Business Agility is NOT

"Your assumptions are your windows on the world. Scrub them off every once in a while, or the light won't come in". - Isaac Asimov

There are many good agile frameworks out there. But 'Business Agility' does not imply that only a certain agile framework (for example, SAFe) needs to be chosen and applied throughout the organisation. An organisation (especially big ones) can adopt multiple such frameworks or in fact implement hybridised versions too. They can even adapt these frameworks or perhaps evolve something of their own (I often recommend this approach when the right enablers are in place). Regardless, the key here is the adoption of the mindsets, values, and behaviours that have come to be associated with lean and agile success stories. Agile for example is essentially a set of 4 values and 12 principles. Ditto for Lean which can be condensed to a basic set of 5 principles. The rest in terms of specific practices, processes or artefacts are all negotiable and context dependent. After all, every organisation is a complex adaptive system and hence the path to Business Agility is unique. In fact, not every part of an enterprise even needs to implement an agile framework in the first place - there is more to Business Agility than just implementing agile methods. Business Agility does not imply that the organisation must apply agile ways of working (say scrum or kanban) in every facet of their organisation. There will be places and scenarios within the same organisation where applying Toyota style lean manufacturing practices for example, is the right approach. While agile is often associated with ways of working in product development (particularly in software development) and lean is associated with repetitive manufacturing processes, both share the same foundational philosophy and it is difficult to imagine an agile business organisation that has not embraced aspects of both. In other words, both lean and agile toolkits are necessary for a business to become truly agile. Relying only on development oriented agile methods and practices will not cut it in most cases. In fact, even traditional (a.k.a. waterfall) based sequential routines might make sense in certain parts of the overall business. There is no conflict in this approach because the idea of enterprise-wide Business Agility does not come with a 'one-size-fits-all' answer or any such expectation of global standardisation. It is holistic, evolves empirically based on what works, and warmly embraces diversity of opinions and approaches along the journey.

Unfortunately, there is also a perception amongst some that agile equates to anarchy. They harbour the idea that Business Agility can mean a free for all, chaotic environment where everyone is always having 'fun' and doing what they want without governance or leadership guidance. Nothing can be further from the truth. Yes, truly agile environments foster 'fun at work' and empowered self-organisation. But like Adam Grant says, "fun isn't an enemy of efficiency, it's fuel for finding flow'. Leaders in these organisations find themselves acting more like coaches than 'bosses' as they painstakingly build up the organisational ecosystem to make self-leadership a reality. Acting and controlling like a mechanic based on a predictive model of the world is not an option anymore - in agile, business leaders act like gardeners and nurture the organisation - knowing fully well that just like gardeners, they are stewarding living systems and cannot predict or control the weather. Gary Lloyd, has written a great book on this idea called 'Gardeners Not Mechanics - How to Cultivate Change at Work'.

Author's Insight: There has been some confusion within agile practitioners in technology that if they are involving a product owner (from business) who has direct access and interaction with end customers, then they are doing Business Agility. Even more problematic, a common antipattern has been calling everything a 'product' and the existence of the 'proxy product owner' - someone from IT (typically a business analyst) who fills in the product owner role neither with direct line of sight to the customer nor any real engagement with the customer facing people in business. But as we shall see, merely overcoming this problem with having a PO hailing from the business or changing the lexicon by renaming erstwhile solutions/applications to 'products' does not equate to achieving Business Agility. These are nothing but window dressing at best.

The Four Agile Values (from the Agile Manifesto - agilemanifesto.org)

1. Individuals and interactions over processes and tools;
2. Working software over comprehensive documentation;
3. Customer collaboration over contract negotiation; and.
4. Responding to change over following a plan

While there is value in the items on the right, in agile, the items on the left are valued more.

In the following chapters we will explore and summarise what a Business Agility journey might look like. But first let us clear the air about a common misconception - agile vs agility!

Agile vs Agility

"It is easier to act yourself into a new way of thinking than think yourself into a new way of acting" - Brian Robertson

Agile and agility are not the same thing.

Agile refers to the new ways of working and being - a set of values, principles, behaviours and practices. While there are multiple frameworks that bring different practices, rituals, processes and behaviours together into consumable packages (and yes there are differences amongst them), they all agree on the same set of basic principles and values of the agile manifesto. Agility on the other hand is the hallmark of an organisation that has truly adopted and matured agile ways of thinking and working. It is an emergent property of a complex, adaptive, organisational system. It is the state when you can say that yes you are now an organisation that is focused on the customer, nimble on your feet, and very adept at adapting to changes. In other words, agility gives you the licence to embrace a VUCA world and dance in step with it. As you can imagine, it is a moving target and there is hardly any organisation that displays perfect agility because everything inside and around the organisation is always changing after all. Perfection may be the enemy of the good but a commitment to continuously improve and a constant striving to achieve it are the hallmarks of a truly agile organisation. In agile circles, this difference between agile and agility is also known as 'small a' agile vs 'capital A' Agile (agile meaning agility and Agile meaning agile practices).

Also, there is a difference between teams merely employing the practices of Agile (a.k.a 'doing agile') vs. teams really embracing the agile values and principles (a.k.a 'being agile'). Teams 'doing agile' are often very visible because they are typically colocated (physically or virtually), do short daily stand-up meetings, use whiteboards and 'post it notes' to track their work together, uphold policies that limit the total amount of work to be done within a certain time interval, show off completed work to their customers at short intervals, and conduct joint learning sessions. Most of these 'ceremonies' do help in embedding the agile values and principles. However, just because these teams are participating in these events does not necessarily mean that they are being agile or achieving agility. What matters is the intent behind the adoption of the practices and the depth of commitment to the agile values (mentioned earlier) and principles (see below at the bottom of this section). Ultimately, it is about these teams (and the organisation as a whole) truly embracing the agile mindset. Of course, it is never easy as the drag and friction of old mindsets and beliefs is usually quite heavy. It must be remembered that it is this 'being' agile element that actually gives rise to Agility (also refer 'List of Corporate Values that emphasise Business Agility' at the end of part VI)

Spotting agility and the lack of:

Various agile maturity frameworks are available to assess how agile an organisation is. In the author's experience, there is a quicker and more

> *informal, albeit intuitive approach that works too - there are certain signs and symptoms that can be quickly picked up by an experienced agile practitioner or coach. For example, are the breakout areas in your company normally empty and your employees always in back to back meetings? Do you see them having lunch on their desks most of the time and are they always saying that they are super-busy with little time to think or consider doing things differently? Are the same kind of problems always recurring in the organisation although perhaps in different departments and in different times? Are the town halls generally quiet and not many people speak up? If these sound like your organisation then you can be pretty certain that even if agile practices are being followed, you are pretty far away from a matured Business Agility state. While Agile is necessary for agility, it is not sufficient! And as we will discover in the following pages, there is a lot more to Business Agility than just adopting agile practices or even being agile in some parts of the enterprise.*

Agility and Scarcity

It may be of interest to note that agility naturally emerges in contexts where overcoming difficulties is a survival requirement. In these environments, the constraints imposed due to lack of resources and structure is simply too much. Take the case of road traffic situation in India or in many other emerging economies - road density is inadequate in comparison to the population pressure and sometimes even abysmal. The sheer unpredictability on the roads can be mind boggling for drivers who are accustomed to driving on smooth, well-maintained roads in the western world (with separate lanes, road-markings, traffic lights, speed limits etc). Instead, what you have there are vehicles, animals, and humans all competing to move forward on narrow roads that are dusty and constantly being dug up for repairs etc. Paradoxically, a linear rule book driven approach will lead to accidents in such a constantly evolving and unpredictable situation. The only way to survive and move forward is in fact to be able to accept the unpredictability without judgement and constantly adapt to the actions of everyone else on the road. Constant one-to-one communication while driving is quite key and achieved by honking horns! ('individuals and interactions over processes and tools'?). The same holds true in the larger economic sphere of emerging markets as there is simply too much variability to be able to survive by following a centrally laid down linear approach. One of the key reasons for the success of emerging economies, despite all the disadvantages and often the colonial inequities they are still saddled with, has to be this naturally developed competency of adjustment and accommodation - a core tenet of agility and now a deep-seated cultural quirk. While visiting India, many foreigners easily spot this cultural characteristic - 'thoda adjust kar lo bhaiya' or 'hey, please adjust a little bit brother' (English translation of the Hindi phrase) is a phrase often heard wherever you go in India. It also leads to a unique type of innovation - 'Jugaad'. It must be said that this quick 'sense and respond' characteristic and finding innovative ways to adjust and cope in order to survive against obstacles and odds is not unique to India. In fact, the whole Lean movement which later evolved and matured into agile emerged from post war Japan when Toyota faced extreme economic shortages and resource scarcities - an alternative mindset needed to be found and staying wedded to the existing structured and Taylor-istic[4] management approaches simply could not work anymore in that environment. Most startups also struggle with scarcity and risk and for them too, survival is the greatest challenge. It does not matter if they are based in a developed economy. They do not have predefined

---

[4] Frederick Winslow Taylor was an American mechanical engineer. He was widely known for his methods to improve industrial efficiency. Production, he contended, was governed by universal and natural laws that were independent of human judgement. The object of scientific management was to discover these laws and apply the "one best way" to basic managerial functions such as selection, promotion, compensation, training, and production - Yonotan Reshef: Taylor's Scientific Management

processes and rulebooks that they must follow and they can therefore make their own decisions on the fly, roll with the punches, and keep moving forward.

> **Important Information**
>
> Focus is a key value in agile. People are encouraged to work on one item at a time instead of multi-tasking. Multitasking sounds efficient but actually leads to productivity loss due to context switching and there is a good deal of evidence to support this (see Chart below). The more tasks you take on simultaneously, the less you can focus on each and the greater is the productivity loss.
>
> | Number of Tasks | Percentage of Time on Each |
> |---|---|
> | 1 | 100% |
> | 2 | 40% |
> | 3 | 20% |
> | 4 | 10% |
> | 5 | 5% |
> | More than 5 | Random |
>
> *From Quality Software Management Volume 1 – Systems Thinking - Gerald M Weinberg, published by Dorset House Publishing in 1992*

> In fact, it has deleterious effects on intelligence too - a study involving more than 1000 workers by the Institute of Psychiatry, University of London found that multitasking can temporarily decrease IQ by up to 10 points, more than twice the amount seen in studies on the effects of smoking marijuana.
>
> Here is what Chanakya had to say about multitasking ~ 2400 years ago :
>
> "Na cala-chittasaya karya-avyaptih" - Chanakya
>
> English translation: *No work completion for one with a vacillating mind.* In other words, if one is constantly changing his mind and focusing on different pieces of work instead of staying focused on one through to completion from start to finish, much fewer items of work will get completed in a given period of time.

The 12 Agile Principles:

1. Our highest priority is to satisfy the customer through early and continuous delivery of valuable software

2. Welcome changing requirements, even late in the development. Agile processes harness change for the customer's competitive advantage

3. Deliver working software frequently, from a couple of weeks to a couple of months, with a preference to the shorter timescale

4. Businesspeople and developers must work together daily throughout the project

5. Builds projects around motivated individuals. Give them the environment and support they need, and trust them to get the job done

6. The most efficient method of conveying information to and within a development team is face to face conversation

7. Working software is the primary measure of progress

8. Agile processes promote sustainable development. The sponsors, developers and users should be able to maintain a constant pace indefinitely

9. Continuous attention to technical excellence and good design enhances agility

10. Simplicity; the art of maximising the amount of work not done is essential

11. The best architectures, requirements and designs emerge from self-organising teams

12. At regular intervals, the team reflects on how to become effective, then tunes and adjusts its behaviour accordingly

Your Business is now Digital but are you a digitalised business?

If your business has survived disruptors and recent disruptions (especially the one due to Covid19), then Congratulations! Chances are that you are already a digital business today or are at least significantly underway. With tougher disruptors expected to emerge fast and many more severe but unpredictable disruptions to emerge, there is little leeway left to not becoming a digitalised business.

It is now common knowledge that the need for digital transformation had started with changing customer needs and expectations arising from access to the internet and mobile devices. Various disruptors emerged in key markets and industries and literally started dominating existing players in a matter of a few years (think Amazon, AirBnB, Uber, Spotify etc.). Many stalwarts fell to their knees and disappeared out of business just in the last decade. Others are trying really hard to swiftly change gears and become a digital business in order to prevent being disintermediated out of existence. Unfortunately change today is less about fine-tuning and optimising and more about dealing with existential threats.

Pretty much everything today is basically a computer, generating humongous amounts of data. This data is making it possible to drive large scale digital transformations. Digital Transformation is ultimately about automating operations, developing revenue-generating digital capabilities, and bringing new conveniences and value to customers (*adapted from Going Digital by Isaac Sacolick*). All with a view to developing a deep connection with the customer in a digital world and being able to serve her (ideally wow her too) where, when, and whichever way she wants to be served. This connection with the customer can be established and sustained by exploiting and generating insights from the data being produced literally everywhere, every second and at scale.

Customers today expect a 24/7 access (think cloud) to your products and services through intuitive interfaces and platforms (without the need for training/ explanations/ support). They also expect quick and regular improvements and updates without having to change or upgrade their purchases every time. They expect your products to integrate and work well with other products and services they are consuming. Finally, they expect you to deeply understand and empathise with their consumption journeys so that you can continuously innovate and come up with the next best thing to satisfy their unmet and 'next order' needs.

So, do you have a cloud first strategy yet? Do you have a digital transformation programme that has started with direct sponsorship of the top leadership team? Are you thinking in terms of products and customer journeys as opposed to projects and features? Are you using team collaboration software as opposed to still relying primarily on emails? Is software and data integration not an issue in your company anymore? Have you started to monetise your own software products? On your road to digital, are you digitalised enough - i.e. are you able to capture the benefits of implementing digital technologies?

Why Agile Underpins Digital Success

"Technology is just a tool. In terms of getting the kids working together and motivating them, the teacher is the most important" - Bill Gates

There can be no success without digitalisation. While many businesses can launch digital initiatives, not all can truly transform into digitalised entities. Achieving a true digital transformation demands a shift to an agile mindset and the adoption of agile work practices across the enterprise. It's crucial to recognize that merely embracing digital technology won't suffice for efficiently addressing shifts in business models, industry boundaries, and the emergence of new partnerships and ecosystems driven by innovative startups and major companies like the FAANGs. Digital transformation and becoming a digitalised business centre around becoming a real-time entity, shifting from mere transactions to building relationships - agile plays a pivotal role in this transition.

To succeed in the digital realm, it's imperative to not only digitise processes but also embrace data-driven and faster decision-making (a key piece in Business Agility). After all, the vast amounts of data generated by digital technologies must be leveraged for rapid decision-making and continuous learning. Additionally, fostering a culture that respects people, working seamlessly without silos and bureaucracy, and engaging in co-innovation with customers and partners are all integral components of this transformative journey and share a lot with achieving long term Business Agility. It begs the question then, can you really become a matured digitalised business with all the shiny new tech bells and whistles without adopting agile principles and practices across your enterprise? Clearly, the short answer is - No!

In a pre-digital world, scale gave cost advantages which is why successful companies massively outgrew competitors over time even if they were slow and less responsive to customer needs. What they offered were standardised products available at scale. Smaller organisations being more nimble and agile could reap the benefits of customer intimacy and continue to flourish in smaller, niche domains. But digital has changed all that. For the first time, agility can be achieved by large organisations without having to give up scale - elephants can finally balance on balls and dance like ballerinas. Being agile and digital, these large organisations are now able to make quick decisions even while tapping into gigabytes of real-time data both structured and unstructured. This is precisely how agile, like the essential engine, underpins and powers digital business ecosystems (where transaction costs are close to zero and network effects extremely powerful). Yes, it is indeed possible for large organisations to move at pace to offer products, platforms and services quickly before they become obsolete and irrelevant. But if large organisations choose not to (survival is a choice after all), then equally, using the same digital technologies, the smaller competitors that had been playing in tiny niches all this while are now able to rapidly gain scale even as they continue to delight their customers and maintain intimacy. As too many digitally native and 'born agile' companies have proven, achieving scale in a digital world is basically free and fast. So, if a large organisation today refuses to adopt agility and prefers to simply implement digital technologies without changing the underlying organisational logic and culture, there is no reason why a smaller company or startup will not quickly threaten and then overpower it. Luckily, several large and traditional organisations are transforming very successfully and showing the way - GE, Siemens, DBS are just some of the names that come to mind.

Author's Special Note: Now that it is clear to see that agile underpins digital success, digitalised businesses should have distinguishable mottos. If you think about it, a digital business has 4 main success criteria - growth in uncertain markets (agile strategy), product-market fit (agile design), time-to-market (agile delivery) and time-to-scale (cloud). So, a generic motto for a digitalised business should sound more like - "we are selling an awesome experience to customers across omni-channels, enabled by scalable and integrated digital technologies, driven by an agile workforce and ways of working". Are you thinking about your business on similar lines?

The Myth of Agile= IT fad

"If your competitor is rushing out a product and you have better technology, it's not good enough to have the better technology. You have to be faster" - *Elon Musk*

It is true that most of the proponents of the agile movement started their journeys within tech companies or in IT departments. Historically, IT for long had been an order taking cost centre and been perceived as a highly expensive bottleneck slowing everyone down. It was a black-box that no one in business really had a line-of-sight into or understood very well. Things started to change in the late 1990s and early 2000s however, and market pressures for speed and innovation necessitated the creation of a nimbler IT function that could develop software faster and better. The existing sequential approach which was defacto at the time (known as 'waterfall' [5]) was not working well

---

[5] Dr. Winston Royce, credited as being the creator of the 'Waterfall' in his seminal paper "Managing The Development of Large Software Systems" never mentions the word "waterfall". The knowledge work world has coined this term. And for good reason. Just like water can't go

anymore to satisfy the new demands for speed and value. Thinkers and practitioners in software development began to borrow and adapt principles and ideas from lean and Toyota's product development approaches (the New New Product Development - HBR) and created new practices that began to be known as Agile. In fact, the Agile Manifesto (written more than twenty years ago in 2001) starts by saying "we are uncovering better ways of developing software by doing it and helping others do it".

But Business Agility is not about a few IT teams doing agile or being agile and developing good, safe software fast (although agile software development is a good thing and very important). Nor is it about a whole IT function doing agile in a scaled-up manner (agile tech services is a very good thing too). Business Agility would require teams throughout the organisation adopting the values and embracing the principles of agile regardless of whether they are in marketing or sales or HR or finance or procurement or operations or legal or any other part of the business. It is a mindset and a way of working in which, to begin with, monolithic work is first broken down into smaller manageable chunks with much greater transparency and accountability around it. It is about people across the enterprise as a whole coming together to actively collaborate and co-create in order to a) deliver value to the customers quickly and b) sense and adapt continuously in sync.

So, will it suffice if only IT starts to think and practise agile ways of working? Of course not! It is very important for business operations, marketing, support services amongst others to benefit from collaboration and continuous improvement for the sake of the organisation's customers. Excellent customer experiences are multidimensional with software being only one of the key pieces. In other words, in most organisations, IT alone is not what the customers / stakeholders are paying for/interested in (even in organisations

---

upwards in a waterfall, the sequential nature of the traditional PM process makes it extremely hard (and costly) for past "phases" to be repeated.

making and selling software products, IT works within the context of the larger organisational environment in an interdependent way). So the idea that agile is only for IT companies or IT departments is nothing but a myth. Business Agility is about the entire enterprise collaborating to continuously uncover better ways of doing business (i.e. hiring better, designing better, procuring better, serving better, selling better etc.) to stay in business and succeed in the longer term no matter how dynamic and unforgiving the marketplace is.

BUSINESS AGILITY MEANS EVERYONE
TOGETHER AND EVERYONE ALIGNED.
EVERYONE ROWS THE BOAT

In fact, organisations where IT delivery team are working in agile ways but the rest of the organisation still uphold age-old Tayloristic management practices and behaviours have become 'feature factories' (i.e. where features and business requirements are being developed fast and efficiently but the customers or shareholders aren't seeing much of a difference). Any benefits that the teams are experiencing are invisible as far as the customers are concerned. In my experience, this is often the case. Many organisations still treat It as an order taking function and they are allowed to carry on with whatever flavour or fad they want to adopt as long as things don't get any worse than they already are for the 'business'. From the CEO or Board's point of view, the focus continues to be very much on annual cost reductions (especially when budgets are tight or external market conditions are not that encouraging). In today's digital world however, as we have argued before, this is likely to be only a short-term temporary phase before the organisation as a whole starts to fail and go down like a sinking ship against a tidal wave of smart modern competitors. An agile IT function as an island in a sea of traditional command and control based organisational ecosystem will not be enough to prevent such a dire fate. If this plays out, then all that will be left behind in the world are a few outsized digitally driven monopolies that started as small entrepreneurial and 'born agile' firms not that many years ago - a new age of oligopoly will dawn. Already, at 3 trillion USD, these FAANG companies comprise 10% of the US stock market (just to put that into context, a market cap of 1 trillion USD is larger than the GDP of 90% of the countries in the world) - is this a sign of the times to come?

THE CRUX OF BUSINESS AGILITY

Fortunately, there is a better way - Business Agility, the crucial lifeline that traditional organisations desperately need today. Yes, the age of digital demands Business Agility from organisations for their very survival. IT functions have already been experimenting with agile for several years now and disruptive events like the Covid19 Pandemic have proven how important it is for businesses to stay nimble and flexible in order to ride out the waves of uncertainty. The looming AI driven disruptions about to unleash is something that no one has ever seen before. The time is just ripe for CIOs and CTOs to have the right conversations with the board and the CEO to a) demonstrate the possible benefits of Business Agility and b) establish a practicable path to get there. In fact, no time could be better because post Covid19, CIOs now have a deeper and a two-way relationship with the CEOs and the rest of the C-suite. There is a new level of trust that has been established and bringing the Business Agility topic into their strategic conversations is the first step to unlock benefits that are almost guaranteed to bear fruit. In fact, COOs, CFOs, and CHROs all have to play a key role in taking agile out of the IT box and embracing it across the whole business enterprise. From an operating model perspective, 'Processes' and 'People' benefit as much from agile as the 'Technology' element - be it in the IT department or elsewhere.

The most important thing to realise is that in the digital age, business and IT are not to be seen as two different worlds. They are actually the same! Everyone is part of "the business" and Business Agility by definition spans across both the erstwhile separate domains. When organisations become agile, the business is not the customer of IT anymore. Rather, there is just the end customer and "the business" developing and supplying the products and services to them (with all technology being just 'business technology'). In other words, through the Business Agility journey, an enterprise's strategy, operational capabilities and technology comes together to meet and align. This is really not trivial.

Business Agility Company Spotlight: MARCUS by Goldman Sachs

Marcus by Goldman is the retail banking subsidiary of Goldman Sachs that was built up as a digital fintech and became a 2 billion business in record time.

According to Harit Talwar, ex CEO and chairman of Marcus who oversaw the creation and acceleration of Marcus during 2016-2021, this business is a poster child example of adopting Business Agility within a larger and in fact, a huge corporate entity (at the time of writing this book GS is a 47 billion USD business with 48,500 employees spread across 80 locations). From idea to launch, Marcus took only 8 months to come out as a new company and ready with its first set of products.

While Marcus adopted all the usual tenets of agile workplaces (like for example formation of agile teams a.k.a agile squads, scrum masters, daily stand-ups, retrospectives, agile tooling), there were a couple of things which distinguished the approach from some of the other typical adoptions seen elsewhere. At Marcus, Harit made sure that the entire conversation of the business shifted to agility – adopting agile was not an option but in fact, was simply table stakes. People had to live and breathe it and 'Business Agility' needed to become part of the DNA. So, the conversation was shifted from 'what do we have to do to adopt agile' to 'what is needed to achieve outcomes in the marketplace'. The entire C-suite bought into the idea because they all wanted to build a modern business and achieve great results in the marketplace. For Marcus, this conviction and commitment of the senior leadership was a big factor in building the new business with 'Business Agility' as its core ideology and operating model. There emerged a common realisation that Marcus had to operate like a Flash-Dance (in which individuals and teams organically generate a beautiful thing by simply staying aligned to the broad objectives and simple rules) rather than operate like an Orchestra (in which all the talented musicians play their bits perfectly by strictly following the instructions of the conductor). The whole organisation was therefore organised around customer journeys and each customer journey had one or more dedicated squads who sat and worked together. Far from being development only teams from IT, these squads were cross-functional – each would have members from various functions like credit, compliance, tech, product etc. and pre-covid when almost everyone would work from the offices, they would have the entire wall dedicated and converted to a huge whiteboard. Standing right next to the whiteboard containing visualisations of their customer journey, work items, issues and performance trends, the team members would conduct their daily stand-ups and other conversations. Leadership would be readily available to the squads on the floor for anything they would need support on. According to Harit, "The human body is truly agile. All the organs and systems in the body work together as a team focused to optimise a single objective whenever called upon to do so – take the example of what happens when you are running for example, or the body is fighting off a disease or infection. Even AI is aspiring to model the human brain, so why can't organisations try to emulate the body?"

Harit also commented that the adoption of Business Agility must be organic and customised to the nuances of the organisation. It should not be implemented as a prescription with all the criteria of a certain agile model being perfectly checked off. He quipped "Progress is more important than perfection" and to me the author of this book, it effectively sums up the continuous- improvement oriented culture that he successfully helped build at Marcus.

Agile in IT - How exactly is it done?

"Innovation distinguishes between the leader and a follower" - Steve Jobs

While Business Agility is the goal and this book is all about that, it will be irresponsible not to start with agile in IT as this is where it all started and is most mature in most organisations. In fact, it is impossible to have Business Agility without the tech function and tech experts within it practising agile ways of working. Also, the lessons that have been learned here over the last twenty years are invaluable and need to be considered before thinking about how to adapt and apply the key tenets across the whole business enterprise. Indeed much has been written and talked about agile in IT by various experts over the years.

At the heart of IT is the application development and delivery lifecycle. It comprises planning, design, development, testing, deployment and operations. In the traditional 'waterfall' model, these have to be done sequentially. Just like water cannot go upwards and backwards in a waterfall, none of these steps can be undone or redone without incurring prohibitive costs. Also, work would be done in big batches, often whole solutions would be built in a single batch and all the required would move together sequentially from step to step (often from department to department). Agile in IT has been largely about applying lean agile work breakdown concepts and practices (like for example breaking down large batches into smaller user focused increments) and then efficiently flowing the work through a 'pipeline'. Initially, the goal was to develop applications more quickly, with less risk, and this is the context in which agile was developed and refined. The focus was on the 'development' pipeline only. In other words, it was in the main, a software development methodology. Over time, it extended to spreading this new way of working over to testing and deployment all the way to support operations and security. Sub-movements like Dev-Ops and Dev-Sec-Ops were born and today the most mature agile IT shops embrace these sub movements. Yes, Agile in IT has now been with us for 20 plus years. Of course, not all of IT everywhere is agile matured - the reality is that many IT organisations are still adopting and evolving it in their backyards and maturity varies from organisation to organisation.

Normally, IT organisations would initially select the digital and relatively self-contained parts of their organisation, form a few self-organised teams (see Glossary) and start agile practices under the guidance of an experienced (and often certified) scrum master or agile coach. Especially, at the start when people do not yet understand or apply agile in the ecosystem, it is usually piloted in a decoupled application because heavy interdependencies with non-agile teams or functions would make it extremely difficult. Whiteboards and flip charts are used as information radiators to bring in visibility which after a while are often supplemented or replaced with software tools (like Jira, CA central, ADO etc.) that are increasingly cloud based for easy remote work. The benefits achieved in a few months to a year would then support the expansion of agile to other teams often as a self-funded initiative. Slowly, momentum would get built up and even legacy platforms and service operations would adopt agile (although success there would require customisation of the approach as what worked in digital will not work if simply lifted and shifted). Teams would typically start measuring things like velocity (see Glossary) and display agile metrics like burndown charts and burnup charts to make progress visible. Impediments, risks and bottlenecks would also become visible. Teams would work in short iterations and conduct regular retrospectives to learn and improve their ways of working based on their own observations as well as feedback received from their customers and stakeholders. Focus would be on finishing work rather than starting work. Focus would also be on prioritising the work better based on what the 'business' considers to be of greater 'value'. Interdependencies with other teams would be made visible and leaders would help eliminate them by changing architectures and operating models. Their role would become much more coaching and development oriented rather than continue as information disseminators or approvers.

As a result of implementing the above, several benefits become visible: relationship with 'business' also improves as they are encouraged to work more closely and are expected to provide frequent feedback to the IT teams. Development times reduce, defects and bugs reduce, number of deployments per period increases, highest value features are delivered first, and overall costs reduce due to reduction in the need for coordination and other non-value-added wastes (lean tools are great at identifying these!). The business starts to feel that the teams and their outputs are now more predictable and of higher quality.

PART II

JUST THE MODELS

Team Level Agile

"Excellence is a discipline, not a performance" - Adam Grant

As per Harvard Business Review, collaborative efforts have increased by 50% over the past twenty years [6]. Agile models may have been a significant contributor because the agile movement has traditionally been about employees actively collaborating with each other and customers to continuously improve value delivery. The smallest unit of such collaborative engagement is the Team. Agile teams are often cross-functional, small, self-organised (see Glossary), and focused on a common goal at any given point in time (which is expected and welcomed to change from time to time). By making work and impediments visible and transparent, agile has promoted team members to become accountable to each other, fix issues quickly, and communicate better with all stakeholders. There is a clear shared understanding of what a good 'finished' work item looks like, 'team

---

[6] Collaboration Overload is Sinking Productivity - by Rob Cross, Mike Benson, Jack Kostal, and RJ Milnor, Harvard Business Review, Sep 7, 2021

agreements' are often in place and trust is foundational. 'Agile' and 'Teams' have thus become synonymous; one cannot think of one without the other.

While both Scrum (as Scrum of Scrums or Scrum@Scale) as well as Kanban have been used successfully in scaled contexts, these are two of the most popular team level agile frameworks. In Scrum, small teams (3-9 members typically) work together with a common vision using a common backlog of work. The highest priority items in the backlog are selected to be worked on first (i.e. in increments) and completed in short time boxes (typically 1-4 week duration) called Sprints. There are only three roles - the Product Owner (owns the product goals, vision, customer liaison), Scrum Master (ensures that the team correctly implements and matures Scrum practices), and the Scrum Team. Most development teams dealing with complex or evolving work are better off applying Scrum as their preferred agile model. The beauty of Scrum applied at a team level emerges from the fact that long lists of requirements which comprise a large complex project can now be broken down into meaningful user-centric pieces, estimated, prioritised, and pulled by the team in small batches to be worked upon and delivered by the end of each Sprint. The team often swarms around these high value 'user stories' (see Glossary) to get them done quickly. Teams are expected to be self-organised and empowered to make decisions. Instead of doing what they are 'told' to do, teams do what 'they' think is the most efficient way to deliver 'value' to the customer and learn from mistakes along the way. Remember, the point is not about having two-week Sprints to process and deliver work faster, rather it is about creating an efficient delivery mechanism so that the team can more quickly find out if there is a problem and adapt more quickly as a result of the feedback. The presence of a PO and often direct access to stakeholders whenever possible makes this possible.

Kanban is about visualising work, limiting WIP (work in progress), managing flow, making policies explicit, implementing feedback loops, and improving collaboration. The whole point being to identify what the individual units of value are and then to optimise their flow back to the customer. For teams adopting Kanban, work continuously flows in and out of the team. Members finish the work before starting another and inventory and queue time is actively reduced or eliminated. This speeds up the overall time it takes to deliver an individual item to the customer and at the same time prevents unnecessary stress or burnout on the team. The work is made visible (almost in real time) often using simple status columns like To Do/Doing/Done. The work can also be categorised into various classes of services ('urgent' or 'expedited' can be a class for example). The focus is less on prioritising and more on maintaining the rate of flow as items get pulled in continuously to keep pace with the rate of demand (a.k.a. Takt). The only prioritisation is - now/next/never. Most operational teams dealing with repetitive and urgent requests are better off applying Kanban as their preferred agile model. It is important that the excess demand beyond the team's capacity be managed in the right way. In the absence of Kanban, excess demand is pushed down, and teams unfortunately get overloaded. This actually not only increases burnout but even decreases productivity. If there are capacity gaps, then Kanban will make it visible and then it is the leadership's job to identify and remove the systemic issues that are causing bottlenecks. There is little option to hide or not take action as awareness shines a bright torch on gaps that had remained invisible before. The team benefits because they can focus on moving the work items quickly and predictably and this is the beauty of Team level agile.

Organisation Level Agile (Scaled-up Models)

"Remaining stagnant is the beginning of the end" - Indra Nooyi

Organisations are traditionally organised in hierarchies regardless of whether these hierarchies are flat or tall. If Business Agility is to be achieved, then clearly, agile adoption needs to move beyond a single team and thereby encapsulate all levels of the organisation. This "scaling-up" of agile and reaching beyond one single team to include a whole department, division, or functional group is what can be understood as Organisational Level Agile.

Compared to very small organisations often dealing with single products, relatively simpler scenarios, and at most a few agile teams, the focus in organisation level agile shifts from simple products or features to larger and more complex products/services that obviously one small team within a function cannot build or deliver. Value can only be delivered now from larger pieces of functionality. It involves the coordinated work of multiple teams (often spread across the globe and nested within the department or division) working interdependently and collaboratively. Trends come and go fast, market conditions change, and even small organisations grow - a few teams adopting agile here and there without scaling-up will not generate the impact necessary to make a dent on market responsiveness.

This is also true for functional products or platforms being built for internal stakeholders. A larger team (i.e a team of teams) with a more diverse set of skills is needed and they need to work on a larger scope. In traditional ways of working, these would typically be treated as a functional or departmental 'programme'. But, with scaled-up organisational agility, the 'team of teams' would be persistent, work on cadence from a single backlog of work, and deliver incrementally. Together, they would of course aim to deliver bigger chunks of work (perhaps called 'capabilities' or 'features') rather than smaller items like 'stories' or 'tasks' that an individual team would deliver. The opportunity in scaling agile this way lies in achieving greater alignment, economies of scale, dependency reduction, and generating shared knowledge. Teams can ensure that they work with each other and not against each other - in other words, working like a true team of teams. In traditionally run organisations it is all too common for silos within a division to compete with each other over turf and for projects to compete for resources based on political clout, coercive power, etc. rather than the ability to meet long term divisional goals. With scaled-up agile, goals and objectives set at a higher level can now become more meaningful for individual teams through cascading down the nested structures and can generate a shared purpose for everyone. Working from a common backlog of priorities becomes a reality thereby ensuring removal of conflicts and earlier delivery of value.

For scaling up, multiple frameworks are available for guidance, and these are constantly evolving to implement scaled agile successfully in large organisations. Some of the popular ones out there include SAFe, LeSS, DAD, Scum-at-Scale, etc. - each often comes with its own terminology and role definitions. Many organisations have now benefited from these models to achieve amazing results. Certainly, a few have faced challenges too. However, as we will explore in 'Inviting Everyone to the Party' in section IV, this is mainly because change management remains somewhat of an art, and not every organisation consistently excels in implementing change in general and new ways of working/thinking in particular.

Individual Level Agile

"All life is an experiment. The more experiments you make, the better. What if they are a little coarse, and you may get your coat soiled or torn? What if you do fail, and get fairly rolled in the dirt once or twice. Up again, you shall never be so afraid of a tumble." - Ralph Waldo Emerson

Individual level agile underlies all other levels. Ultimately it is about how an individual thinks and behaves that determines how they will collaborate with other members of the organisation regardless of whether they are part of the same team or not.

It is very important that every individual working within an agile team understands and adopts agile values, principles, and practices. It is undoubtedly a two-way street. While it is possible to 'comply' with agile ways of working in teams without personally and psychologically investing in it, that invariably leads to tensions and conflicts causing personal and team level stress. Becoming agile as an individual is obviously a process as it involves unlearning old behaviours and habits and embracing new principles. It involves learning agility and embracing a growth mindset. It allows skills and people to flow seamlessly to where the most value can be created (more on this concept later in Part IV where we talk about building the infrastructure). As more and more individuals become adept at being more agile, the teams and organisations they work in also become more agile over time and the organisation culture changes. This is the golden key for making agile stick in the organisation.

Companies that are committed to Business Agility cannot afford to overlook this key piece of the puzzle. As Peter Drucker famously quoted, "culture eats strategy for breakfast". The best toolkits and models of agility will only go so far unless each individual is transformed. So, keeping a close eye on the pulse of the individuals who make up the organisation and nudging them along the journey is quite important in developing organisational agility. And this is exactly where honest one-one coaching can work miracles which is why agile coaches and scrum masters become invaluable on the road to Business Agility. Also, a large part of middle managers' job now becomes coaching (more about middle managers in Part V, under 'Just the Gotchas').

Unfortunately, sometimes some individuals will find it hard to make the transition despite the best efforts of the team, the coaches, and the leaders. Some of them will reluctantly comply and some will actively resist or try to sabotage. These are typically people who were the 'alphas' and their individualistic self-image is deeply associated with acting as the lone hero. They can find it very hard to become truly agreeable and work well in a real team-based construct. There is a lack of will to change and a few are simply uncoachable. It is therefore an important duty for management in organisations aspiring to embrace Business Agility to identify and support these individuals in a manner that ensures they don't hinder the progress of agile.

But it must be understood that individuals adopting agile is not just about mindset or belief. It usually includes adopting and adapting agile practices (often used by teams and teams of teams) to suit the individual. For example, while Scrum usually timeboxes work periods as one week to four week Sprints for teams, at an individual level benefits can also be had with Sprints that last just a day. Planning, delivery of increments, and reflection all happen within a span of hours rather than weeks.

End-to-End Agile (Scaled-out Models)

"Alone, we can do so little; together, we can do so much" - Helen Keller

If Business Agility is to be achieved, then agile needs to "scale-out" from merely a development team (or a team of development teams construct within a department or function) to encompass the entire chain of value flow - right from the point of customer need identification (i.e. the point where costs start to accumulate) through to value delivery and consumption (i.e. the point where revenue starts to flow in). This may include not only customer facing business groups, marketers and designers, but also operations people, security, HR, legal, architecture, etc. as may be necessary (of course depending on the context).

While scaling-up addresses the development of a relatively large chunk of functionality that can't be created by a single team, here we are talking about building and delivering a complete end-to-end product, service, or experience. Unless this 'scaling-out' is done and achieved, 'scaling-up' or 'organisational agile' will not on its own give rise to Business Agility and the customers will not feel a big difference. This is often a point that is missed in many failed agile transformations especially because the pressure to carry on with existing structures and mindsets is strong. Scaling-up largely retains the pre-existing organisational roles and structures - the focus is often reigned in to stay within departmental and organisational boundaries. The idea in scaling-up is to gain some agility while still implementing agile on an existing hierarchical structure originally created to control work, workers, and manage conflicts. You get one or more vertical functional silos each doing scaled-up agile. Overall therefore, it results in suboptimization and only partial achievement of the benefits of agile. Inter-departmental dependencies continue to exist and PMOs (Programme/Project Management Offices) are assigned the impossible task of managing these. Of course for them It becomes a constant Whack-a-Mole exercise and agile can seem like a new source of frustrations. Scaled-agile then gets the blame as being ineffective in generating step change in enterprise-level performance.

End-to-end agile ensures that the emphasis shifts from narrow focus on a part of the chain of activities (value stream segment) that falls within a particular function or department to the whole value stream (see Glossary) - basically, everything that is needed to start and finish the valuable work end-to-end for the customer. Agile people and teams now organise around the flow of value. It doesn't matter which functions the participants come from, everyone is now part of the same end-to-end value stream (also a 'team of teams' construct but imagined from a left to right, horizontal 'flow' of customer value perspective). Everyone in a 'value area' (sometimes meaning the same as a business unit or business portfolio) is working together to get the service or experience delivered to the customer from start to finish. This can even include staff from suppliers and teams from vendor organisations and third parties. This is indeed how old bottlenecks and delays resulting from hand-offs, dependencies, restricted communications, and lack of cooperation due to political fiefdoms get addressed.

Value streams (called as such or by any other name as the organisation deems fit) can be large or small. Typically, a large operational value stream can support multiple customer journeys but at least one key journey. Similarly, supporting value streams (internal value streams which do not generally have an end-customer touchpoint) can support multiple employee journeys (or vendor journeys etc.) or at least one key journey. In turn, an operational or supporting value stream can be enabled by one or more 'development value streams' as long as the operational or supporting value streams use products that need to be built and serviced. (In case you are wondering, yes, development value streams can also cut across multiple silos within the development area, say IT, and can in turn consume services from shared services groups). The construct may start to sound complicated at this point but remember large organisations are complex and complicated after all. In fact, the value stream lens can enable simplicity because for the first time, you learn to see work the way it actually flows in the organisation (horizontally and zig-zag across functions). Seeing giant pyramidal structures and boxes neatly laid on top of each other on an organisation chart hides more than it reveals when it comes to the actual flow of work.

Regardless of the size and shape of the end-to-end construct, the success criteria now shift to end-to-end lead times and overall outcomes rather than specific outputs and features for which a particular segment or function is responsible for. It matters less how many story points teams have each delivered - instead, what is of greater importance is how much customers have adopted the solution or utilised the service (or how much benefit the business is able to safely obtain overall). Safety and security are also part of the equation and built-in rather than an afterthought with another department looking at the products and outputs before it is delivered to the customer. *Note: Increasingly, this is being done for IT products and this approach of shifting and embedding security earlier in the life cycle is being referred to as 'DevSecOps'*

Scaling-out emphasises the importance of systems thinking and optimising the whole rather than focusing on local performance optimisation. Thinking of all activities and interactions as part of a value stream helps in seeing the whole system and prevents local sub-optimisation. Actually, value streams (no matter how good or bad the flow within them is) exist in all organisations but people do not see it or realise it because they sit in their own silo and take a narrow, vertical, and limited view of the organisation. It is important to realise that these value streams like Russian Dolls often form a nested value stream structure (value streams, sub-value streams, sub-sub value streams etc.) in large organisations. For example, Bank → Investment Bank → Capital Markets → Trading → Equities → Market Making. Each level is associated with corresponding flows and business outcomes. This structure should be identified and made visible to everyone so that every task can become meaningful and purposeful. Identifying the interactions is critical [7]. Tools can help here. Fortunately, many tools have emerged to help in this area. For example, if the sub-value streams are using Kanban, their Kanban boards can be connected and visualised together. At a more strategic level, the flow of entire portfolios of strategic work can be similarly visualised and made accessible to everyone involved with a simple click of the mouse. End-to-end value flow involves upstream strategy and discovery work as much as actual development and support. Obviously, all this was not necessary in a pre-digital world where the leaders and managers (with perhaps help from PMO) only needed to plan the work from start to finish and bark out orders at their workers within their silos to just execute the orders on their assembly lines. People would just focus on the work their function was responsible for and just assume that the whole thing would simply fit together and offer the best outcome to the customer somehow. Such thinking or way of working is a recipe for disaster in the modern, competitive, and disruptive business landscape and Business Agility with the end-to-end model offers useful guidance.

Business Agility for large organisations requires a combination of 'scaled-up' and 'scaled-out' approaches that fit well together. Value Streams do not necessarily replace the need for hierarchy or functional specialisation. Disregarding one in preference to the other leads to problems and friction.

---

[7] Dr. Russel Ackoff: "A system is never the sum of its parts". It's the product of the interaction of its parts"

But again, successful models have been found and refined by many organisations and they provide a good starting point for one's own unique journey. Needless to mention that review and optimisation of organisational structure is therefore a critical variable to make Business Agility take root and mature. More on agile reorganisation will be discussed in the 'Building the Superstructure' section under 'Just the Right Start'. For now, it is worth remembering that trying to achieve the benefits of Business Agility without reorganising/augmenting the siloed structures to focus on customer value will not result in business success. Of course, even value streams do not completely eliminate silos but certainly they can reduce them significantly by making sure that all needed teams are working as one entity without external dependencies. As has been amply argued and mentioned already, Business Agility is not about simply doing agile but doing it in such a way that business success is achieved and maintained. It requires experimentation and constant fine-tuning of the structures and processes.

PART III

JUST THE LEADERSHIP

"Leadership is not the sole responsibility of one person, but rather a shared responsibility among members of an emerging team. An individual leader can accomplish much, but a culture of leadership can accomplish more"
- Mike Myatt, a global authority on leadership

Becoming an Agile Leader

"People are not stupid. They are oppressed" - Eli Goldratt

At this point, the greatest impediment is not the need for better methodologies, empirical evidence of significant benefits, or proof that agile can work outside IT. It is the behaviour of executives. Those who learn to lead agile's extension into a broader range of business activities will accelerate profitable growth. [8]

Business Agility is a team sport in which people work in an empowered environment and feel trusted to freely speak up, do things differently, and make mistakes without the fear of consequences. It is a major mindset shift

---

[8] Rigby, Darrell K., Jeff Sutherland, and Hirotaka Takeuchi. "Embracing Agile: How to Master the Process That's Transforming Management." Harvard Business Review 94, no. 5 (May 2016)

and a cultural transformation for many large organisations. For more than a century, organisations have followed the dominant management philosophy of Taylorism and Fayolism and it is still deeply embedded in many organisations although few would openly admit it. Also embedded is the idea of market fundamentalism in which possessive individualism is the dominant construct - it is assumed that the 'economic man' is greedy, selfish and lazy. Hence, most work is still financial incentive driven and transactional or contractual rather than cooperation driven, purpose driven or collaborative. Business agility turns this on its head. However, this transformation never happens unless the leaders at the top really understand it, support it and set the tone. The way to set this tone at the top is to demonstrate and sustainably role model the new values, mindsets and behaviours themselves. They need to literally personify the principles and live and breathe the values. Unless the leaders at the top become agile leaders, the transformation to Business Agility will not happen - perhaps only some of the practices will be adopted here and there and some so-called "best practice" agile structures will get installed. Ultimately, it involves leaders at all levels of your company shedding some old habits and patterns (like retaliation, blame gaming or working in siloed fiefdoms) that in the larger context really don't serve any real purpose other than just self-aggrandisement. Traditional command and control leadership (if at all this can be called leadership in the first place) on the other hand turns people into sheep so that they can then be goaded or beaten (Oops!) to achieve mediocre organisational results at best. Not very different from the British East India Company that may have invented and perfected this mode of management more than two centuries ago! It worked well for a certain bygone era - that of colonialism and 'divide and rule' by firearms, sword and guile. It will take a very strong advocate to agree that it can still successfully work today (even if significantly watered down and made much less violent).

In other words, if you are the CEO, then agility in your organisation starts with you. Let that really sink in.

"Rajyamulam indriyajayah" - Chanakya, 320 BC

English translation: Enterprise is rooted in conquering bodily senses. In other words, the enterprise cannot be separated from the individual and leadership from the leader. The individual leader must be less concerned about his own sensory fulfilment (indriyajayah is a well understood concept in India and means going beyond one's own selfish goals and ego) and be foremost concerned about the good of the enterprise he leads. This is basically the core principle of what we now know as "servant leadership" and is a critical factor for Business Agility to thrive.

In the digital age, where intellectual capital and organisational capital far outweigh other types of capital (e.g. financial), the key to success is an empathic and people centric a.k.a 'agile culture'. While the goal is to be completely obsessed with customer experience and stakeholder success, this cannot happen if people are continued to be seen as just 'resources' to be optimised [9]. People are people and should be treated as such i.e. adults who can be trusted. In fact, the thing that is at the very foundation of a true agile culture (and as a consequence, of high performance teams) is 'Trust' with a capital T. The choice is really between two belief systems: "It is best to get everything right up-front and we should ensure that this happens most efficiently" and "It is impossible to get everything right up front so we should ensure we are efficient at learning as we go because mistakes and deviations are normal and to be expected". The latter obviously is reliant on trust. So, the real question boils down to how you can as a leader really live and breathe trust.

---

[9] It is mathematically proven and empirically experienced widely that when resource utilisation approaches high levels, waiting time and hence lead times disproportionately increase. This is obviously quite un-agile and hence a balance just be struck. This is especially true when there is variability which is quite common. Mathematically this has been expressed by many including the Kingman's equation.

In an agile context however, trust does not mean blind trust or accountability free autonomy (i.e. letting people do whatever they want without any guardrails). On the contrary, trust means holding people accountable for their learning - allowing people psychological safety (see Glossary), time, and resources so that they do courageously take chances, make the necessary mistakes and actually grow and attain mastery. It means believing that everyone has a great deal to contribute to the organisation's continued success if they are allowed that opportunity to learn and grow. It is about moving away from a command-and-control model where leaders have all the right answers to a servant leadership model (see Glossary) where leaders ask the right questions and offer vision, help, and support. They set the strategic context and provide a purpose (the big 'Why') instead of providing all the answers. It is not about abdicating responsibility or accountability but becoming the 'Guru' who sees and appreciates the organisation as an ecosystem, uses his experience and position to envision a broad purpose, supports individuals and teams on their journey, guides and inspires. In other words, they act as a catalyst rather than the person at the end of a decision chain hoarding most of the decision-making rights (more on agile decision making in Part IV) It also means motivating people with a shared purpose, clamping down on self-destructive competitive instincts and magnifying the collaborative instincts. Of course, the benefits of collaboration will not fully materialise unless diversity and inclusivity are made real in the organisation. Leaders cannot afford to simply pay lip-service to it. Many organisations are now actively ensuring that their workforce profile is sufficiently diverse and once that is achieved, it must then be made possible for everyone to feel welcome and to develop a sense of true belonging. This is what gives power to collaboration. According to some studies, it leads to a 6X improvement in agility.[10]

---

[10] Which Two Heads Are Better Than One, Juliet Bourke, Australian Institute of Company Directors, 2021

This is not some imaginary utopia - it is possible and has been done by organisations that have survived and thrived against the toughest of competitors endowed with deep purses and strong pre-existing strategic advantages. Case in point is Spotify, the audio streaming and media services company (seen as a leader amongst companies that deeply care about Business Agility). It is hugely successful with 551 million monthly active users and 220 million paying subscribers as of June 2023. Daniel Ek, the founder and CEO of Spotify is known to have declared that the only way Spotify could survive against potential competitors like Google and Apple (even before these competitors came and launched their own music streaming services eventually) was by being able to constantly innovate and stay ahead. On many occasions he said "We aim to make more mistakes than anyone else and make them faster" and he often backed it up by saying "by the way, here is the top mistake I made last week". This is the kind of vulnerability, trust and commitment to living the agile values that paves the way to true Business Agility transformation and great success in the marketplace.

End of the day, the product of an agile leader is an empowered, customer focused, and happy team (or team of teams) who make quick decisions that only they are often best placed to make (even if some of them turn out to be wrong ones!). In fact, in a post pandemic AI driven world, the future of work is highly likely to continue to remain remote or hybrid and in such a world, self-motivation is a primary requirement for success. Agile leadership is what can create such self-motivated individuals and teams. When the CEO is able to create such a top team, it cascades throughout the organisation over time and the organisation shifts from a hierarchical brickwork of boxes and solid lines to a network of agile teams and teams of teams focused on value creation and delivery. Again, this can only happen when the leader shifts his mindset from an excessive focus on resource efficiency. That's what worked in the 20th century but not anymore. Unfortunately, many business schools still continue to teach resource optimisation techniques to successive batches of MBA students and put these techniques on a pedestal as if they are the be all and end all of management and leadership theory. Obviously, it can only help develop a certain kind of mindset. In the age of Business Agility, that old mindset needs to shift to a focus on people and value instead. As Russell Ackoff said, "the righter we do the wrong thing, the wronger we become". The CEO can also gain great benefits by truly embracing the concept of teaming up and learning from each other. As per a McKinsey article https://www.mckinsey.com/featured-insights/leadership/the-ceo-moment-leadership-for-a-new-era, several CEOs have found great value during the Covid19 pandemic in connecting with other CEOs within and outside their industry to share experiences and learn from each other in terms of how to deal with the new unexpected situation. This is exactly the kind of agile leadership behaviour that demonstrates to your organisation that team, respect, relationship building and personal learning triumphs over individual bravado and heroics. This is the true and authentic agile leadership that fosters true Business Agility.

According to Peter Zorn, Director Business Transformation at Mercer, erstwhile Talent Transformation & Enterprise Workforce Reinvention at IBM, "such a shift in leadership has already started but it will take some time to really see this as a ubiquitous thing. Some years ago, leaders ran poster campaigns on continuous learning culture and growth mindset but no one really believed that people are the greatest assets. In fact, even now, most are still talking about new ways of working (especially since Covid) rather than talking about 'new ways of leadership'. So how do you teach and bring the senior leadership along on the journey of compassion, communication, and they themselves having to invest the time to learn rather than narcissistically thinking that they know everything? That is the million-dollar question. Very few have cracked it really. As in all transformations, you really need to show people the WIIFM (what's in it for me). Otherwise, the common thinking is 'thousands of people work for me, my life is good, so why should I bother changing?'. But I do see changes happening in pockets (although there are always going to be dinosaurs that are waiting for retirement and refuse to lead in new ways). For instance, there is definitely a change happening amongst the new leaders now in their 30s and 40s. But unfortunately, probably another generation of leaders needs to pass through before all industries (especially Financial Services) truly become pleasant working places where people look forward to coming to work. It's still an evolution and we're a generation away from a place where there is universal respect and inclusion and open mindedness to foster innovation. Another issue Peter sees with senior leaders is that there isn't much of a peer level mentorship going on because they don't know where to find those mentors and they don't even know what they need to learn. However, in organisations operating at the cutting edge of Business Agility, senior leaders have mentors within the organisation - they usually go for somebody young as it is a two-way learning and requires vulnerability on the part of the leaders. These should be done privately rather than being set up as formally run coaching/mentoring programmes. Technology and tools can come in handy to match the two privately and allow self-selection to happen without manual interventions, costs or embarrassments. Also, it becomes extremely powerful, inspiring and vibrant when board members or senior execs individually announce this to the wider organisation and tell stories of how they are taking ownership of their learning and being mentored by staff members regardless of their position in the hierarchy".

Peter is absolutely right. The author believes that as a lean agile leader, you need to be fully committed to continuous improvement and you should make 'perfection' one of your core values. It is indeed one of the five core values of Lean. No one achieves perfection of course but it is the striving that matters. Seeking it continuously will motivate you to question and go past conventional answers in your search for newer, better leadership models and practices - those that are inspired by the agile values and principles. In true agile spirit, the journey to becoming an agile leader is about conducting experiments and learning from them in your specific context as you improve and become a better leader. Without this growth mindset[11], it may become very difficult and almost next to impossible to foster Business Agility. You must therefore be open minded to the possibilities that you don't necessarily recognise yourself. For example, most leaders often overestimate how trustworthy they are. Here again, a coach or the Chief Agility Officer (CAO) can be of immense assistance to help you see some of your blindspots and ingrained assumptions that are perhaps dated and unhelpful. They can pinpoint your non-agile behaviours, get behind your deep-seated beliefs, and analyse the impact they are having on your people - in other words, hold out that honest mirror you truly need to gaze at from time to time. More on Chief Agility Officer in part IV under 'Build The Infrastructure'. *Note: also check the 'leader's alignment checklist' provided towards the end of the book'*

Leading an Agile Enterprise

"Leadership is not defined by the exercise of power but by the capacity to increase the sense of power among those led"- Mary Parker Follett

Leading an agile organisation involves a few basic elements. Firstly it involves becoming an agile leader yourself and then it involves making innovation and continuous improvement a key part of everyone's day job by giving everyone in the organisation the ability and opportunity to think and act like a leader themselves. This ownership mindset and distributed servant leadership is a key component of Business Agility and significantly reduces the leadership lag (described in the Business Agility equation in the beginning chapter).

Agile organisations thrive on relationships. Hence, as a leader of an agile organisation, it is important that you enable the right organisational structures (often informal networks that go beyond the traditional reporting

---

[11] Mindset:The New Psychology of Success - Carol S. Dweck, Ballantine Books; 2007

lines) by waging a constant war against silo formation and politically driven organisational boundaries. Removing such organisation-wide impediments, bureaucratic structures, and other bottlenecks (aka 'organisational debt' within agile circles) should be a top priority. It frees up natural channels of communication and enables collaboration to happen unimpeded as people naturally build and strengthen relationships over time. Equally, leading the agile enterprise will necessitate prevention of the build-up of unnecessary complexity. Every new policy or role or process needs to be thought through and questioned before it is allowed to come into existence. If really needed, then the rationale needs to be documented. This will ensure traceability and when context changes in the future it will be easier to remove or eliminate them. And it should not just be leadership or management who will have the power to review and eliminate these - core to achieving Business Agility is a leadership that encourages employees and teams to self-edit the organisation and its artefacts (e.g. roles, policies, process steps etc.). Of course that requires building and unleashing the 'ownership mindset' across the length and breadth of the organisation. But this is the only way that the 'interest payments' on organisational debt can be reduced or the accumulation of it be prevented.

Another key point in leading an Agile Enterprise 'Decisional Agility'. An agile decision making system must be in place (more on it in Part IV as a dedicated section). The enterprise must stay wary of a disease called 'analysis paralysis' (also see Bezos's 60% rule in Part IV under the section 'Frame the Challenge').

Apart from the war against silos, complexity and analysis paralysis, you as the leader need to establish and communicate "the why' and create the alignment to overall vision and strategic objectives so that people feel that they are working towards a common goal. Self-organised and empowered operational teams do still need something to self-organise around so that they can stay focused on serving the organisation's end customer directly or supporting other teams that do. As a result, you build that elusive agile culture which is so much a distinctive trait of truly agile organisations. Directly working on the culture also helps but only after the structures and enablers are in place to ensure that shifts do not regress back. As a leader you have the privilege of being able to work directly on the culture of course - this is where role modelling, culture hacks, and nudges come into play as effective measures. Building in 'psychological safety' (see Glossary) should be a key focus of these culture hacks. Also, always acknowledge and reward effort and not raw talent - by doing so, you build a learning organisation and help those people with a 'fixed mindset' to take risks and develop a growth mindset. In huge organisations, perhaps the only way to do a cultural transformation is to carve out islands of good agile culture and steadily expose the rest of the organisation to it. Telling (one can think of various types of top down announcements and wall posters) or simply delegating the responsibility to HR, corporate communications or team managers do not work anymore although they still play an important role when it comes to communication. It is as much about role modelling behaviours and gaining credibility by doing what you say. Slowly the tone and types of stories people tell each other in your organisation changes and a new agile culture emerges - one that is open, courageous, collaborative and focused on delivering real value fast.

As a leader it is worth remembering that an agile culture, high performance, and a happy workplace go hand in hand and this is a key outcome you want to catalyse as a leader. Fostering boundaryless relationship building amongst employees is something agile leaders never neglect and offer plenty of personal examples of. This is even more important in today's world where more and more people are feeling isolated and there is a loneliness epidemic gripping many economies and societies. Will your agile organisation and culture offer a ray of hope? Will your company become the best and the happiest place to work in?

> **Research on relationships at work, happiness, health, and performance.**
>
> A study by Officevibe, https://blog.hubspot.com/marketing/workplace-friendships) found that 70 percent of employees say friends at work is the most crucial element to a happy working life, and 58 percent of men would refuse a higher-paying job if it meant not getting along with co-workers.
>
> Many studies including research by Oxford University's Saïd Business School, in collaboration with British multinational telecoms firm BT, has found a conclusive link between happiness and productivity (https://papers.ssrn.com/sol3/papers.cfm?abstract_id=3470734). It found that workers are 13% more productive when happy.
>
> Also consider that researchers at Tel Aviv University studied the impact of co-workers on one's health (https://www.wsj.com/articles/SB10001424053111903392904576512233116576352). They tracked 820 adults over the course of 20 years. They concluded that middle-age workers with little or no "peer social support" in the workplace were 2.4 times more likely to die during the study.

The Idea of Continuous Transformation

"What's dangerous is not to evolve" - Jeff Bezos

Transformation in a VUCA world must be continuous as change and uncertainty is constant. Traditional transformation programmes with long rollouts, heavy processes and burdensome central governance will therefore not cut it anymore and change management playbooks will need to be reinvented. In the age of Business Agility, changes are made proactively and in step with the market across all aspects of the operating model and are never finished or 'done'. By the time the threshold is reached and significant benefits start to accrue, further changes are again required as the environment and market needs have already shifted. Embracing and committing to the idea of Continuous Transformation is therefore a must.

Continuous Transformation however is irrelevant and impossible to achieve unless there is an agile strategy making in place and some sort of an agile delivery capability has also been built. In other words, agile strategy, agile delivery capability and continuous transformation collectively form the tripod on which Business Agility stands. Each is integral and interdependent and none of them on their own can have the kind of impact that is needed. Having a Chief Agility Officer dedicated to the agility effort and tasked with bringing strategy, delivery capability and continuous transformation together is a way to demonstrate serious commitment to the idea.

<u>Agile Strategy:</u> This is about how to constantly stay in tune with the market and sense new opportunities and threats both at enterprise level as well as for individual markets and regions (for large enterprises). It also involves the ability to recognise signals (even weak ones) and run quick simulations, scenarios or mini experiments to explore potential impact. Agile principles of collaboration, empowerment, customer value etc all come into play for agile strategy to come to life. Planning horizons become shorter, alignment becomes real, and everyone participates in strategy making, not just the CEO and the C-suite. Strategic planning departments in large organisations start to think and operate differently (to be discussed in Part IV in the section titled 'bring everyone to the party'). In essence, all strategy making becomes completely infused with principles of agile. This relates to and strengthens 'market sense' in the Business Agility equation we mentioned at the beginning of the book.

Agile Delivery Capability: This refers to the enterprise's ability to swiftly implement new strategies, projects, or products. Much of the core ideas of agile discussed in this book and in most other books on agile relates to this topic. Key concepts include Sprints, User Stories, Backlog, CI/CD (in software delivery), ceremonies such as Retrospective, Big Room Planning, Agile Artefacts, Test First approaches, and Iterative Prototyping. In scaled contexts, it includes Scrum of Scrums and Agile Release Trains (ART).

Continuous Transformation: This represents an organisation's use of agile strategies and rapid delivery capabilities to enact ongoing internal shifts. It involves continuous, cross-cutting changes over longer time frames implemented incrementally. It requires keeping ears to the ground with short feedback cycles into delivery as well as strategy to ensure that learnings are quickly incorporated into the operating model. This is what really builds the resilience muscle at every level (individual, team, organisational and end-end).

Continuous transformation forms the broadest scope, involving the entire operating model, whereas Agile Strategy and Agile Delivery Capability contribute to this continuous evolution by enabling adaptive market alignment and rapid implementation of changes. It is therefore a critical capability for Business Agility. It leads to creating an organisation acting more and more like an organism - all organisms have an inbuilt sense and respond capability. Whatever comes in the way of quickly delivering high value to the customer is taken up as problems to be solved to get to the next target state of better flow of value. Leadership still plays an important supportive and enabling role. Support can take many forms - maybe changes are required in how partners are currently assessed and qualified, or in certain enterprise-wide policies or maybe in how funding decisions are to be made for new innovations to see the light of day. The specifics do not matter but what matters is that these changes that are required to be made across any dimension of the operating model are quickly identified, prioritised and enabled. Traditional organisations wait until it is already too late or simply make it a part of a large traditional programme of work with long timeframes and high risks of failure.

Teams embracing continuous transformation thrive on a clear understanding of the organisation's purpose (the big Why). Confidence in leadership's consistent support, backed by cross-functional and persistent teams, fuels this transformative journey. Doubt arises when these elements are absent, and this leads to scepticism about completing the transformation. Complexities like numerous departments, personnel changes, and decisional bottlenecks hinder progress, reflecting organisational friction, a rigid waterfall mindset, or inefficient information flows.

<u>Author's Special Note:</u> Continuous transformation is exactly where many organisations struggle and hence achieving Business Agility becomes a difficult task for them. For them, operating model change is often by definition reactive, big and heavy. Starting late, they often already know what needs to change (because competitors have already implemented many changes over a period and moved on leaving behind a trail of clarity in hindsight). It is a simple rule after all - just follow what the industry leaders did. Transformation requirements can simply be collected (often blindly copied and retrofitted), packaged into a planned programme of work and pushed down for implementation using a tightly controlled traditional waterfall model. Unfortunately, there are three problems with this - a) Big changes like this takes much longer to implement (mainly due to interdependencies and the fact that many things need to change) b) Resistance is always a given due to factors such as change fatigue, change being pushed down rather than being pulled c) by the time changes get implemented the market has moved on and much of the time and effort expended is of no value anymore. The only thing it does is buy more time before an eventual crisis or collapse ensues. A useful agile concept to adopt when it comes to continuous

transformation is the 'Transformation MVP' [12] and the 'Transformation Sprint'[13]. One of the ways to successfully implement Continuous Transformation is to take the Transformation MVP approach and embed multiple pilots and Transformation Sprints within the Transformation MVTs.

---

[12] A Transformation MVP (can also be called Minimum Viable Transformation or MVT) is an agreed set of minimum changes that is still comprehensive enough to result in a significant benefit for the organisation and/or its customers. It is a readily adaptable and lightweight chunk of a larger overall transformation - be it a total business transformation, or a digital transformation, a functional transformation or any other type. It prevents boiling the ocean and also generates quicker ROI for change. It also leads to lessons learned and course corrections if needed. One or more pilots may be included in a Transformation MVP or MVT and an iterative 'test and learn' element is built into the design of an MVT.

[13] A Transformation Sprint, according to its developers Haydn Shaughnessy and Fin Goulding who came up with the term, is a 6-step process implemented within a timeboxed 4 weeks Sprint period. It is a templated approach that takes into account typical transformation related problems and offers a quick way to get from A to B.

PART IV

JUST THE RIGHT START

Frame The Challenge

"Well begun is half done" - Aristotle

You would agree by now that Business Agility can bring in huge benefits to your organisation as a whole. It makes your organisation better, faster, stronger and safer. It can also identify and heal the fractures and faultlines that might have started insidiously as a result of the digital disruption going on all around. But no successful transformation is ever about boiling the ocean and nor is it about transformation for its own sake. A strategic orientation and decisiveness on which exact challenge you will target at the start is of great significance. Unlike an 'agile adoption' (i.e. implementation of practices and tools within teams and departments) which may require detailed road maps or plans, Business Agility should in fact be a key element of the overall strategic play of the enterprise. At a minimum, it should therefore answer the big 'whats', clearly provide the 'intent' and enumerate the guiding 'principles'. Ideally, the short to medium term objectives and key results should also be put in place and these should again be focused on those that have maximum strategic relevance. In essence, the challenge should be framed with specific business outcomes and objectives in clear sight. As objectives evolve, so should the trajectory of the transformation journey and the key results that the journey should be milestoned by. All key results ultimately should map back to business outcomes like revenue, cost, risk etc and to the broader purpose of the organisation. *Note: Originally introduced as a concept at IBM by Andy Gove, Google has done a great job of turning this concept of creating alignment into a discrete practice which is now being emulated by many others in industry - in agile circles, it is known as OKRs (Objectives and Key Results)* (see Glossary).

While your organisation will evolve and pivot many times and shift gears to focus on different areas of opportunity during the journey, good Business Agility transformations will generally start with a laser sharp focus on only a few (and often just a single) challenges and perhaps only within a certain encapsulated part of the organisation. Especially for big organisations, only a small slice of the larger organisation should be selected for the first few experiments. A good advice here is to go for an end-to-end slice if possible (cutting across all the layers of your organisational cake rather than just picking out the cherries on the top layer or indeed only the base layer) - this may take a bit more time investment upfront but will significantly reduce the overall duration when it comes to scaling Business Agility across the enterprise.

A common and related mistake is to not consider the specific circumstances of your organisation and instead start hastily with a copy and paste approach to agile transformation. No organisational baselining is done, no pain points and opportunities are systematically identified. Typically, the way it plays out is that a senior leader reads about a successful agile transformation in the business press and then goes about targeting all the results achieved by that transformation (often achieved over several years but missed in reading the fine print) in his own company. The tendency is to try and do too many things simultaneously in the hope of getting quicker and bigger results. To take the

Cake metaphor, the tendency is to take out too big a slice. This is tantamount to framing the challenge too broadly (and vaguely). Alternatively, also not unheard of is the approach of too narrowly focusing only on a tiny slice within a business area and thereby failing to achieve demonstrable results that will catch people's attention and keep them motivated. This is the ultra-cautious approach aiming to minimise damages from a new and therefore 'perceived-to-be risky' approach. Good discretion and expert advice (often external) during this initial phase is of great value. Once agile muscles are built and experience is accumulated, it becomes much easier to fully rely on in-house leaders and teams to make judgement calls on what will work best when it comes to choosing the next challenges. As in any good strategy, success lies in choosing your challenges and choosing them well.

Agile transformation across the enterprise can also be done following a more exploratory, fully experimental approach without a clear 'why' and 'what' but it takes much longer and hardly guarantees strategic success in the market. What does sometimes happen is that organisations start with such an approach but realise their mistake and start to give it a proper direction in order to reap the benefits. A case in point is Diageo. Diageo is in the business of premium drinks with over 200 brands sold in 180 countries and 30 thousand employees based in over 135 countries. Darren Faraway, Head of Agile Transition, explained that "Diageo viewed Agile as a transition rather than a transformation. It did not start with an end in mind or a deadline to chase. The company knew they needed agile but not exactly sure why they needed it - there was a driver for change which they felt agile would bring, and they were open to experimentation. Even the Head of Agile role was created simply as a temporary fixed term contract role initially. It is only after we started the journey that specific goals and milestones emerged, and great initial results led to the realisation of the long term importance of the agile role. It came to be seen as a strategic initiative that would run for months and years. An approach was formalised consisting of 3 phases across 8 areas and they all needed to move forward together as one unit. The first phase was simply a phase for finding the high level agility blockers, building product aligned teams of teams and setting the foundations within the agile workforce. The second phase was repeating this to a point where most product development and delivery (but not all) was subsumed under an ART (Agile Release Train - see Glossary). Third and final phase is about embedding a culture of Continuous Improvement. This is ongoing and this is where further benefits can be found from that agility, the type which make companies really profitable and competitive in the market - but you have to pass through the first 2 phases to get here"!

Having seen successes and failures from the trenches, recommended steps to start would be to a) select a key challenge that is currently preventing you from achieving the business results you want, b) achieve clarity on the end state (Vision of what good will look and feel like) c) defining the non-negotiable principles d) identify measurable success criteria (ideally a combination of leading and lagging indicators (see Glossary) e) build a hypothesis around what agile interventions and approaches might best address the challenge given the current state and f) cordon off a section of your organisation where you will start the experiments and focus on the human element of change as you begin. It must always be remembered that Business Agility is only the means and not the end. Achieving the right business results to ensure survival and sustainable success in the marketplace is the end - Business Agility only removes or at least effectively addresses the challenges and blockers to achieving those results.

<u>Author's Special Note:</u> Maybe time to market is a big area of concern because faster and nimbler companies have set foot in your strategic niche and are quickly churning out newer products and services. Perhaps your organisation also wanted to develop them but was too slow to get them off the ground and into the customer's hands. Maybe you build a hypothesis that lack of collaboration across groups and teams is the key issue because of which work-

streams and functional groups are not coming together to deliver the solutions quickly enough - arguably brilliant ideas are not seeing the light of day soon enough. If this is the case, then you should decide to start an agile initiative laser focused on getting cross-functional teams that are able to self-organise and use the right collaborative organisational constructs and tools to sync-up and deliver on a common cadence. As part of this agile initiative, they will then need to be trained, coached and empowered to be able to generate quick learnings with a 'fail-fast' growth mind-set. These would then become the priorities and a clear vision be established and communicated out (doesn't need to be perfect - go with the 40-60 rule of Jeff Bezos [14]). In the same breath, the right success criteria must be selected and be brought to life through a small set of easily trackable key measures to ensure that organisational or team level impediments can be identified early and removed. Simply starting a copy-paste agile initiative with a general construct and generic milestones will not yield the results you want for your organisation. No organisation, context, or challenge is the same - as a wise old saying goes - 'you never step into the same river twice'.

Build the Infrastructure

"In all things that are purely social, we can be separate as the fingers, yet one as the hand in all things essential to mutual progress" - *Booker T. Washington*

The architecture of enterprise-wide Business Agility is built on a foundational infrastructure. This infrastructure consists of certain critical structures and systems. While this foundational layer also evolves over time and adjusts, pieces of it need to be in place right from the very start.

---

[14] Bezos recognised communicated as a matter of principle and practice in Amazon that waiting for 90% information for making a decision is too slow. Instead, Bezos encouraged making decisions with only 60% of the information so that windows of opportunity do not get missed.

A Business Agility Office (BAO) is one such critical infrastructure component. Headed by an experienced Business Agility practitioner (Chief Agility Officer or Chief Agile Coach), this office is the key facilitator to bring the whole enterprise into agile ways of thinking and agile ways of working bit by bit. They work with leadership and operational teams to create a strategy for the agile journey, keep the transformation on track, remain watchful for incipient antipatterns, and prevent entropy from setting in. They keep a watchful eye to identify the bottlenecks (these invariably emerge along the way) that slow down the transformation and are empowered to deal with them appropriately. In fact, the CAO works directly with the CEO to ensure that the agile strategy is an integral part of the organisation's core strategy and touches all aspects of the organisation, not just IT. Agility must be embedded into the operations and DNA of the business. It is therefore important that the CAO has a background in business but experience in technology and credibility amongst IT leaders too. A person with an entire career built inside the IT department may not always have had the breadth of experience in business operations to be able to engage and embed Business Agility across the length and breadth of the enterprise. This is not a point to be ignored when finding the right person for the role. The BAO also plays a key role in busting myths and ensuring that cultural antibodies to Business Agility are identified and managed appropriately. They ensure that agile experiments proliferating across the length and breadth of the organisation actually add up to something of overall impact. One of the biggest problems in change is that change is seen as a project and as a result fights for priority (especially with respect to the availability of non-dedicated teams and employees). A dedicated BAO ensures that the right people are included and their inputs are sought. The BAO should also include people from "organisation change management" as they can bring in a unique and valuable perspective particularly if they are trained and experienced in agile ways of working. But the BAO itself and all other people in the enterprise will also rely on two other key components of the infrastructure.

Modern <u>collaboration and agile working tools</u> that are easy to configure are also critical for success with the transformation and form the second piece of critical architecture. People and interactions across silos or geographic boundaries are key to Business Agility and unless employees and partners can collaborate freely and virtually, Business Agility will suffer. Modern (often cloud based), automated tools widely available today make this much easier and simpler. An early choice of tools based on long term growth expectations across the enterprise will avoid future issues with respect to mutual incompatibility, unnecessary costs etc. According to Peter Zorn, Director Business Transformation at Mercer and erstwhile Head of Organisation Transformation and Client Centricity at Deutsche Bank, "we will no longer be concerned where someone is working and we won't need rigid policies to get people into an office x days a week. We will also see the continuing rapid development of collaboration tools that will bring technologies of AR & VR front and centre - so the current 'Zoom experience' will be greatly enhanced to make it more like we are there in the same rooms as our colleagues and clients"

Installing an effective <u>data, communications and governance system</u> that makes transparency, alignment, and data-based decision making possible is the third critical piece of infrastructure. This will make purpose palpable, feedback fast, and knowledge and learning shareable. I have discussed earlier why agile underpins digital. But the corollary is also true: a solid digital landscape and capability, especially when it comes to being able to effectively create, store, and flow accurate real time data to the point of consumption goes a long way in powering agile. It brings a kind of transparency and trust that is so critical to true agile ways of working. But was unheard of and almost impossible to achieve even just a decade ago. Similarly, it's the only thing which makes skill gaps visible, growth and career progression possible, and a continuous improvement that can be actually tracked and measured. Some kind of talent platform that truly enables people and sets them free on a continuous growth journey. More on this below.

In an interview with the author, Peter Zorn, whom we quoted earlier, explained that having a Talent Management Marketplace and the ecosystem around it was a key factor behind IBM's turnaround from an almost bankrupt company ten years ago to becoming a huge 60-billion-dollar (revenue) company and the world leader in continuous learning and enterprise-wide workforce reinvention. These are the hallmarks of an organisation well on its way to achieve true Business Agility and resilience. According to Peter, 'skills' is the keyword, and the flow of skills and people is the key concept behind Business Agility. This can be achieved when Transparency, Visibility and Personalisation are accepted as core principles across the enterprise. For people to truly want to come to work and engage (how can you have agility without engagement and motivation?), people need to be able to see where they are today and how to get to the current and future roles they want to grow into. Transparency of skill requirements across all roles and positions and learning pathways leading to them is therefore a non-negotiable element in this if leaders truly want to achieve agility and retain employees beyond a few months or years.

The Talent Marketplace being driven by data, enabled by AI and human centric, also allows widespread visibility - there is little point if say the 50 hours invested by an employee to learn a new skill on the TM platform is not visible to the recruiters and those who need those skills! And finally, personalisation is even more important - policies at IBM empower employees to learn whatever they like. Every employee is deemed to be the CEO of their career. With the transparency of roles and skills across the enterprise and almost Netflix-like AI driven recommendation engines, they are able to easily choose the learning that is best for them. The marketplace being much more than just a learning platform, also matches people and enables experiential learning - after all, learning through online videos and courses accounts for only 10% of the journey to effective learning. People can quickly identify and align with colleagues and teams that are already adept and regularly use those targeted skills as part of their day job. They can then invest time in short term practical assignments in those teams, shadowing the staff at work, or even engage in group discussions/ coaching and mentoring. This fosters a type of mobility that leads to retention because you can access and tap the vast opportunities that are usually there in every large and growing organisation. Similarly, when there is some kind of emergency, you can't rely on old fashioned ways and keep calling your mates to discover the right skilled people who need to be teamed and deployed. AI powered, data driven, and human centric again comes to the rescue - the platform makes it visible who's got the skills, where they are, and what they are wanting to do next in their careers. The result is true resilience against all sudden changes in the environment be they internal or external. IBM has 400,000 ppl and everyone is on the talent marketplace, working and sharing across countries and borders. It shines a light on every person in the organisation. Just learning statically on your own has no value unless you can flow and move around to develop and share your learning and skills. And it must be understood that it is not just the tool or the platform - it is the entire ecosystem - policies, skills libraries, culture etc. It is this that enables IBM to massively save on costs of recruitment, achieve quicker time to market, generate higher engagement and improve risk profile (existing employees have already done mandatory training etc and are better aware about protecting company reputation etc).

Build the Superstructure

"It always seems impossible until it's done" - Nelson Mandela

The agile superstructure is the agile organisational model that must be built and refined over time. Business Agility relies heavily on structure in order to flourish. It may be true that culture eats strategy for breakfast[15] but a true agile

---

[15] Actually, Peter Drucker never said this, it is one of the most enduring and catchy misquotations.

culture will be difficult to grow and flourish without a structural framework to grow upon. In fact, even an agile infused enterprise strategy will mean nothing unless an agile operating model is in place to implement it on the ground. True to the principles of agile, this superstructure should be bendy and flexible, not rigid and fixed. The lure of scale and promise of low cost (often only a broken promise due to 'hidden factory' costs mentioned elsewhere in the book) of traditional functional structures must not be mistakenly allowed to outweigh the advantages of speed, innovation, and employee engagement. Bottom-up collective intelligence must be maximised and in this, structure can really play a big part by being built around agile's 'minimum viable bureaucracy' principle. Essentially, what it refers to is a structure that is neither too rule based, inflated and slow nor one that is too laissez faire, anarchic or unpredictable. Governance absolutely has its due place in Business Agility after all (although the proportion of self-governance is significantly enhanced). This well-balanced superstructure is far from being a static target though and by definition will need to constantly evolve and adjust to such opposing forces as those mentioned above. As we have discussed before, continuous transformation keeps the agile superstructure agile and in sync with the needs of the market, available technology and people's aspirations and goals.

We have seen before that agile relies on a multiskilled and/or cross-skilled team-based construct rather than independent isolated departments throwing over batches of partially completed work across the fence to each other. I have also discussed that by definition, Business Agility needs to go beyond the borders of IT and needs to encompass the entire enterprise end-to-end. In other words, it needs the formation of multiple 'teams of teams' that are aligned to the overall strategy and goals. In large organisations, it needs a vertical 'scaled-up' approach as well as a horizontal 'end-to-end' ('scaled-out') approach based on the idea of concepts like 'Lean Value Stream'. A shift in focus from functions and tasks to products and services is also entailed. Many organisations are increasingly finding product based structures to suit them better as they scale their Business Agility journey. Roles would have to change too - particularly the roles of middle managers. This is easier said than done in large traditional enterprises wedded to hierarchical structures for decades if not centuries and still heavily influenced by Fayolism and Taylorism. These are places where the mindset is still dominated by command and control and a culture of reflection is absent (more on middle managers and their role in Part V). This is the reason why small start-ups or mid-sized organisations are able to achieve Business Agility much more easily and much more speedily compared to old established big companies. But this restructuring in big organisations is doable and indeed must be done. As in the cover picture of this book, even big elephants can be taught how to be flexible and nimble and balance themselves on a moving ball (not promoting the practice of keeping wild animals in captivity but remember the circus elephants of the yesteryears!).

Is it going to be easy? - No. Is it possible- Oh yes, absolutely! In fact, this restructuring must be done in an agile incremental manner rather than in a top down big-bang style (more about this in the next section titled - 'Use agile to implement Business Agility Transformation'). Traditional OD (organisation design) approaches with their emphasis on top down and big bang will find it very difficult to successfully design or implement such a nuanced superstructure.

Another interesting fallout of the reorganisation will be the impact it will have on the systems and IT architecture of the organisation. As has been noted and explained by Metcalf's Law, systems will increasingly become modular and de-coupled in order to reflect the changes in organisation structure. Even today 70% of Fortune500 companies operate their core businesses on mainframe systems that use 60-year-old programming languages according to research by Forbes.[16] Similarly, legacy applications and systems still anchor

---

[16] 'From Shopping To Space Travel, How The Mainframe Changed Our World', Pat Toole, April 8, 2014, Forbes

and slow down the pace at which many organisations can move. Reorganisation based on agile principles will bring to surface these hidden issues and root causes and force the right changes required on the architectural front. These changes are often long overdue. It is a virtuous cycle - systems will become more resilient and that will in turn also accelerate Business Agility.

Every organisation's journey will be unique but at the end of the day, there are some good patterns and recognisable characteristics that will be quite easily discernible when looking at the organisation's structure. Bottomline is that for Business Agility you would expect your organisation to evolve into one that looks and feels much more like a living breathing organism than like an industrial machine. A big enterprise would likely end up having thousands of entrepreneurial, networked, self-organising, small teams; lots of coaches; and far fewer managers and centralised groups. Governance mechanisms would be built into the work processes and automated (if possible) instead of being episodic, hierarchical and backward looking. As a visionary business imbibing and maturing Business Agility, you would not only recognise that top heavy hierarchical structures are slow and costly but also realise that a large part of traditional management can indeed be transitioned to self-management through the Business Agility transformation.

Also, In a VUCA world, it is networks that create value and not hierarchies. For inspiration consider Amazon where Jeff Bezos, the CEO, created thousands of, what he called 'two-pizza teams' that are small enough to be fed by a single large pizza (or two small Pizzas). Or, consider Haier which transformed from a traditional hierarchical company and now has over 4000 cross functional and autonomous teams and 2000 self-governing units. Its core value is 'zi zhu jing ying' which translates to 'independent operating units'. With 70,000 employees and revenues of 32 billion USD, it is one of the top 10 most innovative companies in the world according to BCG. (see 'Your Strategy Process Needs a Strategy' - BCG, Nov 14, 2018 and 'Haier Elevation'

- Doug Kirkpatrick, bsuinessagility.instutute, March 1, 2019). Or, why not consider Morning Star Company, a large market leading, capital-intensive corporation whose sprawling plants devour hundreds of tons of raw materials every hour. In this company, no one has a boss, employees negotiate responsibilities with their peers, everyone can spend the company's money, each individual is responsible for acquiring the tools needed to do his or her work, there are no titles and no promotions, compensation decisions are peer-based. Over the past 20 years, Morning Star's volumes, revenues, and profits have grown at a double-digit rate, claims Rufer. Industry growth, by contrast, has averaged 1% a year.[17]

Author's Special Note: Unless you are a digitally native organisation, the evolution to a fully networked agile operating model will take time. Since you do not want to (or actually can't) restructure this top-down, what is important is to lay down the design principles and direction of travel. 'Simplicity of Organisation' and 'High Bandwidth Human Interaction' should be the guiding values to derive the principles. For a large organisation, this will likely involve the transition from a traditional hierarchy to a networked model through a 'dual operating system'[18] in which both the hierarchical construct and the loosely coupled network of teams and 'teams of teams' will co-exist. This is a good thing because it will allow you to enjoy both the efficiency of the hierarchy as well as the speed and adaptiveness of the network. Over time of course, networks will learn to become more efficient too and that is the outcome you would want to aspire towards.

---

[17] First Let's Fire All The Managers, December 201,Harvard Business Review, Gary Hamel
[18] 'Accelerate' John P. Kotter, Harvard Business Review, Nov 2012

The author has developed and conceptualised a 'Business Agility Tree' as a visual metaphor to internalise the key elements of Business Agility. (illustration overleaf). In it, the successful, high-performance, agile organisation is depicted as a tree. The soil, rainwater, and sunlight represent critical elements for the tree's (i.e. organisation's) success: The "Soil" in this metaphor signifies the mindsets and culture. Just as healthy soil provides essential nutrients for a tree's growth, a positive and supportive culture nourishes the Business Agility Tree. It includes values, beliefs, and behaviours that promote collaboration, respect, innovation, and adaptability. A strong organisational culture provides the foundation for agile values to take root and flourish. The roots of the tree obviously depict the agile values. The trunk is the bulwark and represents the triad of autonomy, mastery and relatedness - the three key human needs and motivations that when satisfied gives the strength and foundational power to sustain the tree. The branches represent the various principles of Business Agility. Leaves (each representing an agile practice) emerge from its corresponding branch. The branches also in turn bear the fruits (the business, customer and societal outcomes). But again, none of this can happen without the rainwater and sunlight. "Rainwater" symbolises the continuous learning and adaptation within the organisation. Just as rainwater nourishes a tree, insights, knowledge and learning are essential for the organisation's growth and resilience. And rainwater comes from "Rain Clouds" which symbolises the failures that are so essential to generate learning and insights. "Sunlight" represents purpose, clarity, and vision. Just as sunlight provides energy for photosynthesis in a tree, purpose, clarity and vision energise the organisation. All these come from Strong leadership represented by the "Sun" in the visual metaphor. It ensures that the organisation is heading in the right direction, while a clear vision guides its growth and

> development. These elements play a crucial role in supporting the agile values (roots), motivating the workforce (trunk), applying agile principles (branches), implementing agile practices (leaves), and achieving successful outcomes (fruits) in an agile organisation. They create the conditions necessary for the organisation to thrive, adapt, and continue to produce successful results.

Business Agility Tree

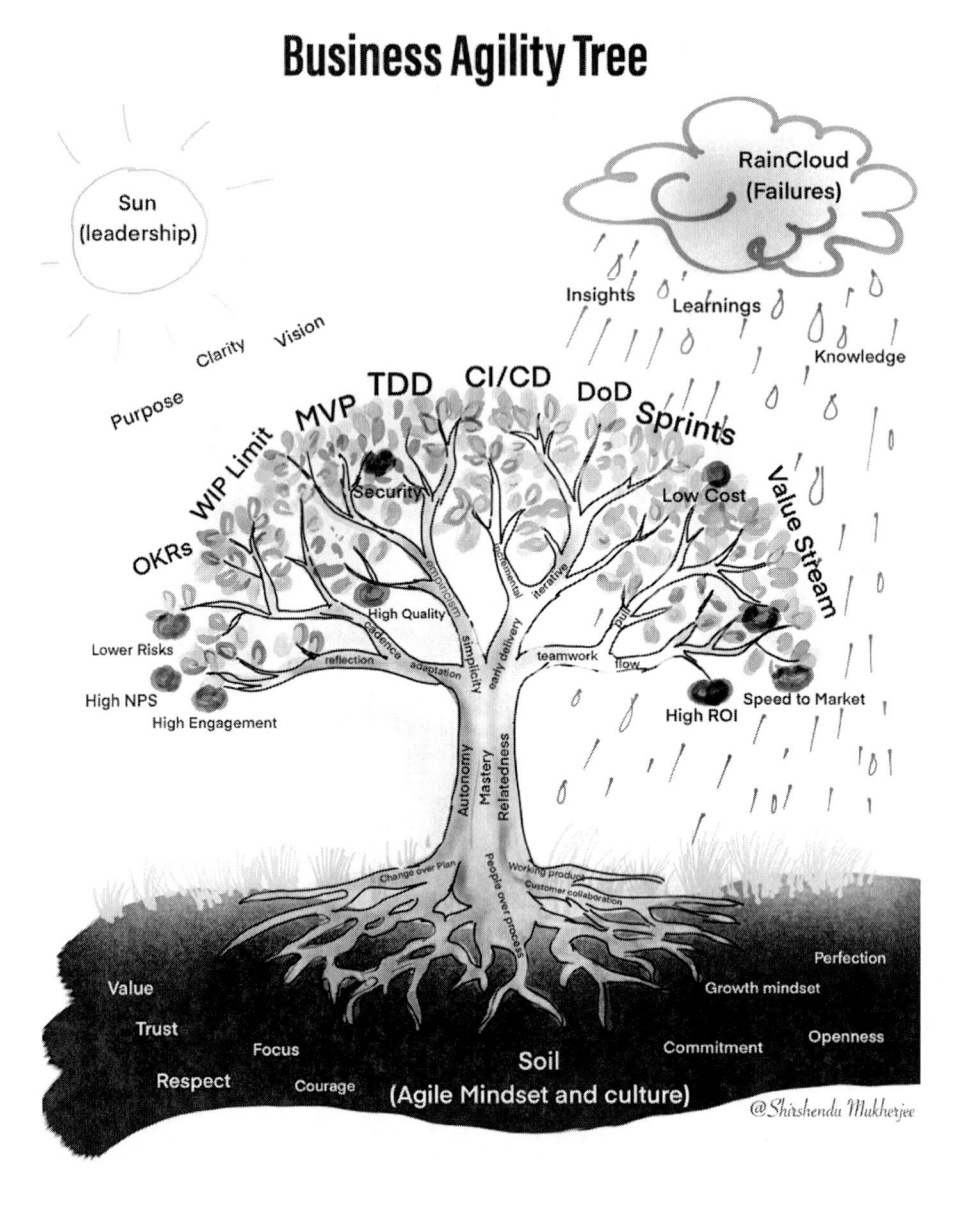

Business Agility Company Spotlight: GIFFGAFF: Voted as the network of the year by the public both in 2021 and 2022 (Uswitch rankings), Giffgaff is a well-regarded mid-sized mobile operator in the UK (a wholly owned subsidiary of Telefonica UK).

One of the key reasons that GiffGaff is successful in the market and is looking to grow even better is down to the effectiveness of its agile transformation. It takes pride in challenging the established ways and improving things by harnessing the power of its people. Like most organisations it too started at the team level and achieved top end status when it comes to success with the well-known technical agile effectiveness measures (i.e. DORA measures like cycle time, change failure rates, number of production releases per year etc). It did not stop at a team level implementation and operational level measures though – a movement from 'projects to product' led to the identification and formalisation of 26 product (teams) that are aligned to 7 value streams. Under the stewardship of John Tanner, Head of Agile Delivery, GiffGaff, and his team and in true spirit of 'Business Agility' these value streams are now being enabled to have full representation of all people involved in the 'end-to-end' value delivery (including functions like marketing). According to John, apart from the wider inclusion of people in the value streams, there are two key things that have really accelerated the journey to Business Agility for Giffgaff.

Firstly, Giffgaff made a conscious effort to streamline its goals system. The OKR system was initially plagued with complexity and fuzziness. There were almost 100 goals at the top and middle level although there were only 7 business areas and value streams. Leadership had no way of seeing whether and where the company was making significant improvements to capitalise on evolving opportunities. Teams were confused about what to prioritise and constantly new measures and objectives got pushed on to them without due regard to available capacity. John succeeded in eliminating the confusion – rigorous analysis and discussions led to retaining just 7 goals (aka objectives) that all teams in Giffgaff now align to. A 'No List' was also implemented to prevent unnecessary and disruptive goals and changes to seep through without due diligence and prior agreement. The C-suite now loves the clarity achieved and the teams love the fact that the OKR based goals system is not just another 'management reporting' initiative but something that really helps them to improve as a team. Regular conversations held weekly and monthly is a key feature of the system and ensures that the discussions and decisions are data and fact based.

Secondly, Giffgaff has been making strides in measuring and installing a generative culture. Taking cues from Dr. Ron Westrum's research on how information flows are indicative of organisational culture, they have developed an in-house framework (see the Science of Agility section of the book for more on the theory) to qualitatively assess the prevailing climate existing at a team level. It rigorously analyses things like cross-team communication types, communication effectiveness, information flow gaps, dependency intensity etc. The outputs are depicted often through the usage of symbols rather than hard numerical measures. These are also aggregated for company level trend / directional analysis. But in true agile spirit, inter-team comparisons are completely avoided – something easier to do when hard numbers are not involved. This again is making Gaffgaff a hard to match competitor in the telecom space where large traditional companies are struggling to be as nimble or as adept at achieving 'Business Agility'.

Agile Decision-Making Engine

"When your values are clear to you, making decisions becomes easier". - Roy Disney

The success of an organisation ultimately boils down to the quality and timing of the decisions it makes - big ones that it makes periodically as well as the thousands of small ones it makes throughout the day in different nooks and corners of the enterprise.

The real underlying reason why traditionally run organisations have been failing is because their decision-making structures and processes have failed them - these are too slow and weak to cope with a fast-changing VUCA world and a new generation of employees who expect more and expect different. The adoption of Business Agility principles and practices strongly helps in treating this ill-suited obsolete decision-making system and infuses it with new health and vigour.

Can you think of the key decisions that large organisations need to make for staying in business and furthering their success? As a senior executive, many of these probably cross your mind - strategic investment decisions, market expansion and diversification decisions, mergers and acquisitions, capital expenditure planning, product portfolio decisions, pricing and revenue decisions, talent acquisition and development, technology and innovation investments, operational efficiency and process optimisation, marketing and branding, customer experience, risk management and compliance, supply chain and vendor management, crisis and contingency decisions, partnerships and alliances decisions, regulatory and legal, performance evaluation and strategy adjustment, exit strategies, succession planning etc. An agile decision-making engine significantly improves these decisions and generates impact not only in the marketplace but also inside the organisation.

Let's take succession planning as an example. Companies use it to pass leadership roles down to another employee or group of employees, but the process is usually not very agile or efficient and the decisions made are not always very effective. This is a key reason why new CEOs and leaders often fail in their job within their first 24 months[19] and CEO succession remains sort of an esoteric art in which luck is perceived to be a big factor. The Great Resignation made headlines in 2021, with thousands of employees leaving their jobs. But another crisis is looming large: the upcoming executive labour shortage as baby boomers leave the workforce. Many are now in the upper echelons of major corporations, including executive positions and are retiring in large numbers. Even the youngest baby boomers will turn 67 by the year 2030. This imminent exodus means that many corporations will have considerable gaps in their leadership team. Hence, succession planning is a critical area now. How could Business Agility improve decisions in this area? A robust 'backlog' of high potential successors could be created, time-boxed 'Sprints' could be run continually to decide appropriate development goals and to iteratively adjust succession plans, 'Retrospectives' could be held on cadence for continuous constructive feedback, the development path could itself could be modelled on agile principles focussing on building adaptive servant leadership, collaboration, innovation etc., assignments could be based on pair-programming principles in which top talent rotates through important leadership positions and are mentored closely. The entire process could be owned by the CEO herself acting as the 'product owner' and the executive team plus the top talent candidates empowered to provide inputs and make decisions along the way.

While adopting Business Agility automatically infuses decisions with new superpowers emanating from the agile principles, values and practices, the organisation's decision-making engine can be looked at and improved

---

[19] Successfully Transitioning To New Leadership Roles, Scott Keller, McKinsey Quarterly, May 2018

separately as a sub-system too. It is to be seen as a shared capability that runs across all value streams within the enterprise. First of all, the decision-making processes and hierarchies need to be identified and mapped. These then should be deployed in a network across value streams in a defined manner - for example, ARTs (Agile Release Trains) could be defined, and specific decisions could be delegated to them. Specific ceremonies like Big Room Planning could be designed to further formalise the types and timings of certain decisions. More tactical decisions could be formally delegated to agile teams and again specific ceremonies and events could be put in place to bed-in the concept at the team level. Teams are enabled with agile metrics (few but impactful) that they can track live. More strategic decisions could be targeted at a portfolio level and certain teams and structures like Value Management Office, Centres of Excellence etc. (see Glossary) could be set up for making or contributing to certain decisions. Visioning and developing Objectives and Key Results with leading indicators becomes the norm as opposed to management by hundreds of KPIs. Overall, and at every level, decision making becomes more participatory, and data driven - stakeholders across functions or geographies become key contributors and appropriate models like Cynefin framework or Vroom-Yetton-Jago model get utilised to decide on the correct approach. All decision outcomes get monitored almost in real time and reviewed if early trends indicate need for adaptation. In fact, the goal of the entire decision-making framework becomes continuous and quick adaptation. And for the first time it feels as if you are looking through the windshield as opposed to looking at the rear-view mirror.

A related idea is that of agile meetings. Decisions are often inextricably tied to meetings, so the question is how do meetings need to transform for the agile decision-making subsystem not to be weighed down by the legacy of old-style meetings? The problem with old style meetings is that often they get in the way of real productive work, and no one really likes them. Many organisations now are in fact trying to reverse this - and beginning to mandate 'no meeting

Fridays' or 'no meeting Wednesdays' (Shopify is a great example of this[20]). But in agile, we need people to interact and ceremonies to be held. We hold this in high regard because we recognise the value of trust, coaching conversations, and participatory decision making. So, the key is not to eliminate meetings but to make them productive and likeable. You will not mature on Business Agility unless your meetings become time-boxed, agenda driven, collaborative, respectful, blameless, data-driven and action-oriented. Also, carefully consider the participants - in other words, do not have anyone invited to a meeting unless they are actually needed (According to a recent study[21] in 2022 by Professor Steven Rogelberg at the University of North Carolina at Charlotte, attending noncritical meetings is estimated to waste about $25,000 per employee annually). People should also have the freedom to refuse a meeting if they feel that they cannot contribute or cannot take actions. Also, the agenda for regular retrospectives should include the discussion on how meetings are going - which ones still make sense and which ones need to be revamped or eliminated.

Use Agile to Implement Business Agility Transformation

As should be amply clear by now, unlike traditional transformation programmes, Business Agility transformation is a journey. This is why some agile coaches and practitioners do not even like to talk about 'Agile Transformations' and would rather simply use words like journey, quest, endeavour instead. After all, it is not about doing agile as a programme with a fixed start and finish date, following a fully predictable path along the way and being done with it at the end of it. Traditional milestone-based approach where you plan the work and work the plan will not work because while the

---

[20] Shopify's CFO explains how its new meeting cost calculator works, and how it will cut 474,000 events in 2023: 'Time is Money' - Fortune, July 14,2023
[21] The Cost Of Unnecessary Meeting Attendance, https://20067454.fs1.hubspotusercontent-na1.net/hubfs/20067454/Report_The%20Cost%20of%20Unnecessary%20Meeting%20Attendance.pdf

immediate outcomes are known and long-term vision established, the steps to get there will evolve depending on what is working and what is not. Unlike leadership mandated change programs where every step and deliverable is planned out in advance, in this case, it is a complex progression - the teams will determine the best route map while the journey is still on. In fact, in extremely fast changing environments, even the strategic vision will evolve through iterations (albeit less frequently) perhaps year to year. The fact is that for a complex system like an organisation operating in a complex environment, it remains unknowable how specific changes will impact the rest of the organisation and what exact effects (both positive as well as negative) will emerge. Such 'emergence' is natural and to be expected from any complex system- biological, physical, or socioeconomic. The route must be continuously designed and quickly executed step by step with continuous feedback and regular updates to the plan based on empirical evidence. Not much different from the core precept of agile philosophy at all.

This kind of change is not 'pushed' by management but rather readily 'pulled' by teams of employees who feel more and more engaged and start to operate in step with and at the speed of the market. Obviously, trust from the leadership team that such an approach will work and is right for the organisation is at the starting point of such a journey. While this trust will increase manyfold as the organisation adopts and matures agility over time, as a corollary, it is not a great idea to start the transformation unless leadership first gains the conviction to go for it. The worst thing that can happen is an agile transformation that is started for the sake of all the benefits that agile promises but is shoved down the throat of employees in a command-and-control manner. Governance and monitoring should also be just enough and lightweight- the idea here is to help teams align and progress together at a pace that is natural and sustainable. Of course, the speed of the transformation accelerates but that is again due to learning taking place and impediments being removed and not because some externally determined arbitrary target must be met somehow. That would be something far removed from the values that agile fundamentally preaches. In fact, Without the values and principles, agile practices on their own don't mean much and such a transformation fails to produce the very results that it is aimed at producing. They end up as just another faddish transformation that costs much in terms of time, money, and anxiety but generates only limited benefits. Agility then gets a bad name and future attempts to implement agile culture and ways of working become extremely challenging.

The agile community of coaches and experts that have experience of Business Agility tend to agree that a good way to get started is to invite voluntary participation. Start with leaders who are willing and have the influence to excite and rally people around them. Under guidance from the Business Agility Office and the Chief Agility Officer, let them collaborate with other such leaders in a value area (or two) to come up with the priorities, the high-level blueprint and the pilot criteria. Most pilots will involve multiple teams and this cross-functionality and collaboration is only to be encouraged. As also, the failures and the tweaks that will be needed to achieve the targeted outcomes. The outcomes and the measures that will track them are absolutely critical to gain the credibility and support of the larger organisation.

<u>Author's Special Note:</u> One thing to be wary of is to introduce too many metrics to measure the success and progress of the agile transformation. While no one can deny the importance of metrics and governance for any journey (agile or not), metrics have the potential of being gamed or to generate behaviours that are not in line with agile values and principles. This can only slow down the transformation at best and derail it at worst. The BAO and CAO with the experience and support of the executive team will need to carefully plan this out and be actively looking out for unexpected consequences or behaviours. Also, it is okay if targets on transformation metrics need to get adjusted as learnings take place along the way - the key is to strive for aspirational targets (meeting them, failing them or overachieving can all happen and to be expected)

Business Agility Means Inviting Everyone To The Party

In a previous section I have already mentioned end-to-end agility and the need for scaling out. Taken together, the end-to-end customer journeys, the operational, supporting, and development value streams that power them, cut across and involve almost every function and department of the enterprise and the geographic regions it operates in. Hence, it is important that every department and function in every geography adopts and embraces the mindset, principles and practices of agile for the enterprise as a whole to achieve agility. It involves collaborating together seamlessly to navigate uncertainty and change. While the journey must start small, it should still encompass one or more vertical slices of the enterprise. And that means that right from the word go, a good approach is to have at least a few people (from different functions and departments) come and actively participate in the experiments and Transformation Sprints that need to be conducted. Soon, many more people from across the enterprise will also need to be invited and over time a point will be reached when the approach will gain a momentum of its own and pull in participants from far and wide.

This is a key perspective that is kept at the centre of the Business Agility strategy. In fact, I would argue that there can be no Business Agility unless the whole enterprise gets engaged in the agile movement. It is one thing to do agile transformation in IT or even extend it out to business in a cursory way by involving them and asking them to become product owners or product managers (see Glossary), but it is quite another thing altogether to do Business Agility. The Business Agility Office for a starter of ten will ensure that no one gets left out. In fact, unless customer-facing business units get onboard, they will hamper even the normal evolution and maturing of agile within the development and IT support functions (if mini agile journeys and experiments may have already begun in pockets within these functions). Of course, getting everyone on board is not easy. But some organisations have attempted it successfully and they have found certain ideas useful in their context which I will share now in this section. I will talk about some of these functions and shed some light on how they can play a part in enabling Business Agility in the enterprise. I will also mention some of the benefits they can themselves gain if they themselves adopt agile ways of working internally.

According to Harit Talwar, ex CEO and chairman of Marcus by Goldman Sachs whose story we have covered in the book earlier as a Company in Spotlight feature, it was certainly not a cakewalk. The most challenging bit was getting the people from different functions (who all had very different backgrounds and perspectives) to talk and speak the same language and understand each other's views. What made it happen was the focus on the common 'why' – right from the outset it was made clear that the enterprise level objectives would always trump any functional level objective. Also, while squad level (i.e. team level) productivity and predictability would still get generated by agile tooling, squad success would get measured and rewarded based on achieving business focused overall outcomes – customer satisfaction, risk scores, cost etc.

<u>Author's Special Note:</u> For agility to really bed in, functions will need to gradually get restructured to align better to an end-to-end Business Agility deployment. An agile operating model with networks and teams of teams will emerge. But it is always a good idea for them to start practising some of the basics of agile behaviours and see the benefits first hand even within their existing operating models. Each will often start its journey with a champion working closely with the BAO and leadership team to draft a vision, success criteria, and create a backlog of agile practices and changes to be implemented and experimented with. Let us explore how some of the key functions within organisations can approach agile and enable Business Agility.

Strategic Planning:

Business Agility transformation should be designed to a) enable agile strategy design and b) build capabilities to deliver and execute agile strategies. By making individual parts of the enterprise connect and collaborate better, Business Agility enables great strategy making - through enabling the enterprise to sense the market and the internal dynamics (including emerging competencies and constraints) sooner and better. This is because people are working in nested teams, are focused on customer needs and sharing knowledge and information as they collaborate to work for the same purpose. This is key to making the right decisions when it comes to 'where to play and how to win' (the two core questions of Strategy).

Agile for Strategic Planning: for Business Agility, strategic planners must move away from extensive analysis and detailed long-term projections to much shorter time frames. Also, the focus now should therefore be on providing the strategic context rather than all key decisions having to be made at the top by strategic planners (executive leadership, planners and external consultants). In other words, strategic decision making should also become participatory, and this is in fact a key component of decisional agility as explained elsewhere in the book. After all, new agile organisational constructs (discussed earlier in the book under 'Building the Superstructure') and readily available data plus modern analytics platforms now provide advanced capabilities for such effective decision making to happen lower down - faster and closer to the customer. Therefore, the mindset and thinking must first change amongst the strategy makers. Many of them already know that they need to change their ways to think and act agile. But most need help in making that change happen. It is not enough to have simply 'executive coaches' at the top - the Chief Agility Officer (CAO) and the Business Agility Office can play a significant role in providing this 'business coaching'.

For example, a good agile practice to adopt by the strategic planning department could be the 'Strategy Sprint'. The Chief Agility Officer with his team of agile coaches can greatly help in supporting its adoption. It can be a great approach particularly when strategy making feels frustratingly slow and difficult and it all seems to go into endless loops without clear agreements. The 'Strategy Sprint' is a way to make 'strategy making' iterative and incremental and feedback is core to this agile approach to strategy making. The steps roughly look like 1) A truly cross-functional team is formed; 2) they come up with a strategy backlog of a) issues b) assumptions to be tested and c) strategic moves/experiments; 3) select a set of items from the backlog and come up with targets; 4) execute the Sprint activities in a focused manner 5) hold daily stand-ups to discuss progress; and 6) at the end of the Sprint the team evaluates and presents the insights obtained and gathers feedback from the board and other stakeholders.

Strategic Planning for Agility: Strategic planning must become more emergent. Today's VUCA world offers no protection to those organisations who 'set' long term direction and move towards it steadfastly without regard for the market changes that are happening almost constantly and often disruptively in most industries. A long-term purpose and vision is still maintained but the intent might change from year to year and plans should be made for months and quarters, not for years or several years at a time. Capital allocations and divestments should also therefore be made much more flexibly and iteratively. Strategic planning departments in large enterprises will also need to collaborate with the CAO for enabling Business Agility across the enterprise by identifying and helping build the right capabilities - it is a two way street. Ultimately, the right business capabilities need to be built or improved for the organisation to successfully compete. These must be identified and initiatives to enhance or transform them must be planned. Then, a short interval based cadence should be set to review progress and identify new capabilities or opportunities to improve.

Finance:

Finance for Business Agility: Business priorities do not wait for the annual planning cycles - they evolve and change especially for an organisation trying to march in step with its market. Unless strategy, planning, budgeting and funding are equally flexible, Finance invariably becomes a bottleneck and a challenge for end-to-end delivery of innovation and services. For achieving Business Agility, the focus needs to shift from departmental annual goals and targets to how Finance enables a dynamic strategic plan. In this regard, a quarterly budget (with longer horizons recognised only as rough estimates and nothing more) is a mindset shift for many organisations. But to be honest, it is really not that different from the way Wall Street also expects to see company performance and results, so, it can work very well with even current norms of external reporting. Employees will need to embrace new ideas (e.g shorter planning cycles), tools (e.g. dynamic forecasting tools), and values (e.g. customer centricity i.e. seeing business as their internal customers or embracing adaptability and continuous adjustments rather than sticking to rigid long-term plans).

Agile for Finance: A project-based financing model with complex cross-charging mechanisms, intercompany expenses (for large enterprises), and unnecessary admin overheads does not help. Finance processes need to be simplified and metrics that monitor flow can be introduced. Introducing agile values, principles and practices within Finance function will enable better strategic investment decisions, greater success rate in mergers and acquisitions, more efficient revenue and cash-flow management, targeted capital expenditure planning and deeper business support through real collaboration and partnerships. Speed of Finance operations would also improve, and the cost of Finance function would reduce.

Marketing:

What will happen if the product development or delivery organisation is working in an agile manner and pivoting month to month to ensure product-market fit but the marketing team is still working to a 6-month plan? Of course, very soon the two teams will be out of sync and potentially working at cross purposes. And, what happens when marketing operates like a bunch of siloes (like product marketing, field marketing, digital marketing, analytics etc) that don't really collaborate together to focus on the biggest common priorities? In both cases, customers will complain or go elsewhere if they have a choice.

Also, marketing work these days is heavily reliant on technology and software. Both end-customers as well as the developers of these marketing platforms are interacting with these software products/systems on a minute-to-minute basis and changes are being made continuously using agile models. Unless marketing also adjusts to this pace of change and starts to work much more collaboratively with product design and delivery, they will struggle to come up with creative ideas for marketing strategies or innovative campaigns and thereby will become irrelevant.

On the other hand, by fully embracing an iteration based, cross-functional model, marketers can engage with customers very closely and thereby ensure continuous customer input and feedback into product design, development and service delivery. By being in the middle, they can really connect strategy, and delivery. The customers sense and see firsthand that the organisation is open to fail fast and learn fast in order to deliver the greatest value to them. This in turn converts customers into brand ambassadors and advocates directly leading to success in the market.

Sales:

Sales is the one area that has for years relied on top-down planning and aggressive individualism chasing competitive targets. How might that need to change when Generation Z and Generation Alpha are joining the salesforce, every data that can be captured from customer interactions is becoming a competitive advantage for upstart competitors, and the delivery organisation is constantly coming up with new and tweaked products/services?

First off, embracing the principles of cross-functionality and collaboration, sales can work more closely with marketing, product development and customer support resulting in a more unified approach to driving revenue and business growth. In fact, sales need to become much more joined up with the rest of the organisation in order to keep pace with all the internal changes that must now be exploited in the market to derive value. They will need to be much more collaboration friendly to accommodate the psychological needs of the GenZ and Gen Alpha.

Secondly, Sales can now use agile ways of working to break down complex sales processes into smaller manageable chunks which will allow iterative improvements resulting in faster time to market and shorter sales cycles.

Finally, they must be able to actively generate and engage with realtime high volumes of market data. An agile approach with clear line of sight to quarterly strategies (as opposed to annual and 5 yr plans), weekly targets, and daily syncs with fellow team members can really work wonders. This will help in being able to quickly pivot to those fleeting opportunities that are short lived but high value.

Human Resources:

Employee experience is the key to employee engagement which in turn is a key outcome expected of agile teams and organisations. HR needs to partner with agile teams almost as members of those teams to enable great employee experiences. Roles, practices, and of course mindsets within the HR team is critical to make this happen. Traditional HR managers become agile coaches within their functions and start to work collaboratively while staying focused on small batches of work. Employees are HR's customers and generating maximum value for them should be at the core of HR's agile vision.

For organisations trying to move into agile, HR departments operating in traditional ways soon get seen as speed bumps. In fact, even some of the HR policies start to get seen as impediments that must be completely revamped. Otherwise, HR, like a bottleneck, only adds constraints, slows decisions, and interrupts the flow of people and skills (this 'flow' is a key feature of organisations achieving Business Agility and has been discussed in Part IV under Agile Infrastructure). Similarly, HR functions, tasks, and processes need to become adaptable to changes and much more efficient and effective at generating value. For example, if the hiring process became much more efficient and made managers and teams really happy about how well their staffing needs were being fulfilled, how much value would that deliver to the organisation? As a result of achieving Business Agility, it is the whole employee lifecycle that can get totally transformed which then directly leads to huge benefits for the enterprise. Finally, Business Agility transformation requires a culture and mindset shift. So again, HR should be right at the centre of it to ensure that the Transformation does not end up becoming just another incremental change effort encompassing only an adoption of new tools and practices. For Business Agility to become a reality and lead to measurable benefits, HR needs to be welcomed to the journey right from the start. The journey will invariably touch people all along the way and in fact, many new roles will get created and new types of structures and reporting mechanisms will get established. HR must not only vet these decisions but also actively contribute to creating them. This will hardly be possible unless HR itself starts to undergo the Business Agility transformation and gathers first hand knowledge of what it really entails. That is the best way that HR can effectively become an accelerator of embedding agile throughout the DNA of the organisation.

Business Operations:

Operations for the most part has traditionally focused on stability, predictability, quality and efficiency. And it makes sense. The Operations realm is often one characterised by elements that are representative of the 'Obvious' and 'Complicated' domains according to the well regarded Cynefin Framework (see 'Not balancing flexibility with stability' in section V - Just The Gotchas). We are mainly dealing with repeatable processes and surprise variation is the enemy. The defects and frustrations that can arise from variation are many - the goal always is to have smooth, frustration free processes that deliver excellent customer satisfaction. This is why lean (including Kanban) with its constant focus on waste elimination and six sigma with its sharp focus on defect reduction (although it must be said that six sigma is much more than just a defect reduction methodology) still remain popular 'go to' methodologies.

As mentioned before, Business Agility spans across the enterprise which not only encompasses creative, knowledge-based work like R&D, Product Development, IT projects (needing exploratory and adaptive approaches) but also flow based operational work which require defect free high volume processing (by machines, operators, or both). In most large organisations, the two must co-exist. In fact, unless there is predictable defect free high-speed work happening on the floor, the business overall will always struggle to ramp up/ramp down fast enough or change direction at will. Unpredictability and variability will otherwise create constant fire-fighting and any planned change will become impossible. In other words, the business overall will not be agile and nimble.

For achieving Business Agility therefore, operations must continue their journey to become even more Lean and take their improvement initiatives to the next level too (say using six sigma or similar approaches). Trying to force fit experimentative agile practices (used in technology development) onto a stable operational realm generally does not make sense in most cases just as automating processes with technology without first simplifying and lean-ing them out is not recommended. On the other hand, it may sound counterintuitive but much of agile has borne out of Lean. Jeff Sutherland, one of the co-creators of the Scrum framework and co-signatories of the 'Agile Manifesto' himself acknowledges this when he says "Scrum derives out of Lean Manufacturing" (see https://www.youtube.com/watch?v=KEu-YEv1LVo&t=10s). The five core principles of Lean are i) Value ii) Value Stream, iii) Flow, iv) Pull and v) Perfection[22]. Both agile and lean share the fundamental constructs of a) remaining committed to delivering customer value, b) constantly trying to reduce time to market (end-to-end lead time) and c) commitment to a continuous improvement cycle. And at the core, both rely on 'visual management' and 'an empowered workforce'. The beauty of Business Agility (unlike agile in technology or product development) in my view is that it embraces both - it accepts the importance of predictability and stability as much as it welcomes change and experimentation.

---

[22] 'Lean Thinking' (1996) - James P Womack and Daniel T Jones

Procurement and Contracting:

Like most functions, Procurement can also become a blocker for Business Agility. Internal processes within Procurement would also benefit from adoption of agile. For example, the onerous and time-consuming vendor selection and contracting processes can be improved from months to days by replacing documentation driven form filling exercises with super quick 'case study pilots' and 'hackathons' in which the suppliers demonstrate their skills and competencies and try to prove that they match the requirements and expectations.

We have mentioned before while discussing 'End to End Agile Model' that true Business Agility requires the enterprise to work seamlessly with its suppliers in a transparent manner. This is what ensures that agile capability in the organisation is truly end-to-end and cuts across all possible silos regardless of whether internal or external. To make this happen, procurement again has a key role to play. Procurement can start with an assessment of its current contracts and prioritise those for which the services being purchased are complex, require innovation, and needs to be responsive to changes in demand i.e. ones where agile ways of working across the end-to-end is critical and immediate. It works closely with product management, delivery teams and suppliers to work out collaborative models of engagement. For these contracts, the focus should shift from heavy documentation and contractual terms of engagement to close collaboration. An outcome orientation driven by overarching goals and objectives of the business and a trust-based collaboration model should be the basis for this new partnership. Vendors become partners and the difference it can make is not trivial. A great example where multiple suppliers and contractors have been brought together to work collaboratively comes from AirBus. According to Luc Henneken's interview in CIO magazine, Airbus deals with more than 3000 suppliers when building out an aircraft platform. Many of them work on a fixed cadence based on Airbus's integration cycles and roadmap using the SAFe agile framework.

Shared purpose, roadmaps, and data ensures that integrations and releases of the platform can happen in weeks and months rather than in years.

Many agile contracting models have emerged because agile does not work on milestone driven sequential flow of work like waterfall does. Also, in agile while we fix the cost and timeframe, we are flexible with the scope to be delivered. Therefore, as a rule, T&M based contracts or Fixed price per Sprint are more amenable to agile working than fixed price fixed scope contracts. Terms and conditions allow flexibility in changing the scope or priorities during the term as well as earlier close of contract if necessary, with a win-win risk shared outcome. To ensure quality and a spirit of risk sharing, the traditional T&M models are enhanced in agile contracts with governance clauses (e.g. required ceremonies, input and output requirements, reporting mechanisms), outcome achievement incentives as well as commercial recourse options if performance or quality expectations are not met, for example. A good practice in the direction of business agility maturity will be to enable a partner to own as much of the end-to-end as possible - this ensures overall accountability for the results and outcomes. It can also work in multi-vendor environments and partners can be motivated to compete on performance and health indicators.

PMO:

PMO (Programme/Project Management Office) functions might do well to understand agile in general and Business Agility in particular because they being the gateway between strategy and execution can play a major role in enabling and evolving Business Agility. Whichever type of PMO organisation they are and wherever they sit in the enterprise currently, they can only do this by truly partnering with the stakeholders (some of the key ones being organisation strategists, Business Agility Office, and Value Stream/Product Owners). For Business Agility to first take root and then evolve, PMOs will also have to ensure that the organisation still performs while transforming because transformations become continuous. Like changing tyres while the car is still driving or repairing an aeroplane while it is in the sky, flying. Many PMO organisations have already understood this and have started a move away from simply being compliance driven 'command and control' project/programme/portfolio standardisation and reporting units to become much more of an enabling and guidance providing entity. In fact, in a digital organisation with agile ways of working taking root and control and accountability getting localised, the PMO is expected to become a much smaller organisation and be centred on facilitation and enablement (within the overall context of the entire enterprise shifting focus from tasks and features to products, value and experience). They help bring the right people together at the right time for timely collaboration to happen across the end-to-end value streams and keep a tab on alignment with strategic vision. They become a servant-leadership-based function and are expected to help with the removal of nutty organisational impediments that are beyond the control of any given team or agile coach. So, in my view, cross pollination, collaboration, and even consolidation between IT PMO, Business PMO, Engg PMO, Change PMO etc.is increasingly a reality which we will see more of as the goal of Business Agility becomes a bigger strategic priority than simply doing agile or adopting agile in the tech function. The other key change will be about how PMO starts to adopt a more holistic view towards governance and risk - not overlooking traditional performance aspects around foundational stability but also nudging in privacy, business ethics, environmental impact etc as key parameters in the mix to keep the organisation in step with changing stakeholder expectations.

One key point about the PMO in agile enterprises is the new tools they need to use. In smaller organisations where the overall products to be built, projects to be executed, or services to be delivered are relatively few, small and self-contained, it is easier to break down the work into smaller independent pieces and dedicated teams can be quickly assigned to work on them 'end-to-end'.

In large organisations however, it is really difficult to eliminate dependencies in practice. So, PMOs will still need to play a critical role in managing them (although the goal and aspiration should be to break or eliminate them). Monolithic reporting tools which only accept data in one direction and in certain fixed formats are being quickly replaced by light weight systems that can work with different types of data sources. Increasingly, these can utilise AI to understand dependencies and generate real time prescriptive and predictive insights for leaders to assess bottlenecks as and when they build up (and address risks as and when they accrue).

Business Change Management:

Organisational Change Management (OCM) practices undergo their own transformation when an enterprise adopts Agile methodologies, adapting and evolving to align with the dynamic nature of agile transformation.

Firstly, the planning, preparation and execution of change is no more for big-bang programmes that happen in one shot at the end of an extended period. Now we are talking about many small changes over shorter periods of time. This obviously implies a huge reduction in change related documentation (as there is no time or need to produce them). A lot of the change activities are now owned by agile coaches whose job it is to ensure that the organisation continuously enables the teams to experiment, change, and function at their best. The Business Agility Office also takes on change management activities. So, a working model needs to be developed on how organisational change management experts and agile coaches can work together with each other and with the 'Business Agility office' to make this play out effectively and efficiently without misalignment.

Also, as an enabler, OCM will continue to play an important role in enabling the adoption and spread of Business Agility across the organisation. Unlike technology adoption, tool adoption, method adoption, process change or organisation structure change, agile adoption will essentially require change at the level of values, principles, and mindsets. Of course, over and above that tool, process and structural changes will also be needed. People will need to correctly understand and appreciate the new way of thinking and working, feel excited, and be determined to make significant changes at a deep personal level. They should not construe it as a 'flavour of the month' fad that will only go to enhance senior leadership's bonuses once implemented properly and 'change orders are complied with'.

Legal, Compliance, and Risk:

As agile is expanded from one vertical slice to another, gradually everyone gets involved and accelerates the journey to full Business Agility. When everyone joins the agile movement, a) IT and other Development teams benefit as there is zero resistance and obstruction to flow of customer requirements through to delivery b) Each function and area benefits because not only do they provide greater value to the organisation but are better able to accelerate their own growth and evolution and c) the enterprise as a whole becomes world class and starts operating at the cutting edge.

Legal, compliance and risk are very significant players in today's industries, particularly regulated ones like healthcare or financial services. By definition, agile ways of working reduce project risks because products, solutions and services get built and delivered continuously in small increments and that way any inherent risk becomes visible and gets addressed upfront. Using agile, risks are continuously identified at the point they arise and they are continuously managed, mitigated or escalated up from the point that they arise. The traditional alternative was to wait for the final solution to emerge after months and years and all the risk was back-loaded by design because initial assumptions and predictions would often go wrong.

With Business Agility, specialists in compliance or risk or legal can play a much better role because of the transparency that agile enables. Also, engagement can be right from the start and on a continuous basis as opposed to engagement being intermittent and driven by firefighting scenarios. Cross functional teams embrace this idea of partnership and collaboration while still respecting independence and objectivity. As a result, business units and customer facing staff can be better supported - for example, contracts can be reviewed and approved in shorter cycles, legal matters can be responded to in a more speedy and compliant manner and compliance assessments can be prioritised and completed faster and in line with the level and timing of the need.

Governance and Audits:

In pursuit of Business Agility, it's crucial to revamp governance processes substantially while upholding core principles. The objective remains stability, predictability and safeguarding assets, aiming to bolster these aspects wherever feasible, all the while ensuring that they don't impede the pace of value delivery. Agile governance can effectively speed up flow within an enterprise and reduce 'Leadership Lag', a key drag factor in the Business Agility equation mentioned in Part I under 'What is Business Agility'. Smaller, iterative risk-based auditing, using cross functional teams for diverse 360 degree assessments, promoting transparency amongst stakeholders, eliminating unnecessary bureaucratic approval chains, using flexible and scalable frameworks for different types of scenarios, and using forward looking metrics, all relying on the core ideas of agile will go a long way to make Governance and Audit an efficient and proactive function. The results will be quite palpable.

According to Parth Joshi, Chief Product and Technology Officer at Hexagon Manufacturing Intelligence, who we have quoted earlier, a good example is the launch of their massive Nexus platform in February 2023, which under normal circumstances would have taken five years to launch had it followed the traditional waterfall stage-gate governance systems and processes. Instead, an agile way of working and governance was used to form and ramp up the team, following an MVP approach (with follow-up releases) for the product. Scoping, staffing, incubation, working with external partnerships, and using daily reviews along with on-spot decisions (vs. months of approval processes) were the key features of this new approach. Another distinguishing feature was the reliance on qualitative feedback and directly listening to people and teams. The leadership team invested in going to the floor and sites and listening to what people had to say rather than relying on numbers on dashboards. The outcome was that a massive new manufacturing platform, Nexus, was released in less than half the time using half the people that initial forecasts suggested.

Enterprise architecture:

At first glance, architecture may appear to have nothing to do with Business Agility. They are there after all to design stability, standardisation, and consistency into the organisation or so the theory goes. However, this could not be further from the truth. EA plays a critical role in Business Agility because a) it ensures visibility on the alignment between technology, process, data and the organisation structure to the overarching enterprise goals and b) it ensures that cost efficiencies are achieved by identifying and removing redundancies. In an agile organisation where teams are empowered and work autonomously, the speed of internal change is swift and continuous. This means that unless EA is working in cadence and maintaining full visibility, governance can fall behind and things overall can get chaotic particularly in large organisations. EA then is always trying to play catch-up rather than being a proactive enabler of a shape-shifting organisation with emergent designs and structures (a hallmark of truly agile enterprises).

By starting with a pilot project, training the team, establishing Agile ceremonies, prioritising backlog items, and collaborating with stakeholders, enterprise architecture groups can successfully adopt Agile and thereby stay relevant in the enterprise.

Celebrate

The road to Business Agility is a long one. We are talking multiple years and for really big organisations, it can even be a decade or more. Also, many of the aspects of Business Agility transformation are counterintuitive and go against the grain of Tayloristic management approaches that have got deeply ingrained over centuries. Consequently, it needs sustained energy from everyone in the organisation (especially the leaders) and lots of support, nudges, and reinforcements. Stopping to reflect on successes (not just mistakes) and celebrating them along the way becomes almost mandatory, therefore. Not recognising successes (no matter how small they are in the overall scheme of things) tantamount to completely neglecting the human dimension and current understanding of how human beings stay motivated. Celebrating initial successes and giving them as wide a publicity as possible is a key step in starting your agile transformation right. This will reinforce the leadership messaging that Business Agility is really important and embracing it is the right thing to do.

One caveat to be aware of is we define success as achievement of outcomes and not progress towards outcomes. While achievement of outcome is based on actual work completed, progress is nothing but someone's opinion based on an assessment or report. An agile mindset prioritises due recognition of actual working product or solution and value delivered over documentation and progress reports.

Here again a Sutra written by Chanakya is enlightening:

"Siddhasya iva karyasya prakasanam kartavyam"

English translation: Only the completed work should be made known (announced). In other words, a manager should talk about planned work only after it is successfully carried out.

Business Agility and Artificial Intelligence

There is no doubt that AI is going to revolutionise every facet of work and life and be a game changer when it comes to humanity's evolutionary journey. While the technology is still quite nascent, it is worthwhile to explore its applications and near to mid-term ramifications when it comes to Business Agility.

First of all, it is a no-brainer that AI will take automation to the next level - repetitive tasks will be the first ones to become obsolete and this will free up human potential to focus on activities requiring critical thinking and/or creativity. In fact, even weak and rudimentary AI can go a long way in making this happen. This will unleash motivation in the workplace and enterprises that are ahead in the journey to Business Agility will be able to tap into this immediately. There will be more focus on the quality of human-to-human interactions (opposed to tools and processes, which is aligned to a core value of agile), mental health will improve and there will be even better work-life balance. Much of human learning will also be supported by automation and AI driven prompts. It will be just-in-time and just-what-you-need. Traditional enterprises will struggle to generate value from this freed-up potential and hence might straightaway go into a headcount reduction mode further increasing the performance gap between the Agile organisations and those that are not. Perhaps a leisure driven economy will also take shape at some point and create whole new markets for a new generation of agile startups catering to satisfy virtual and surreal experiences that people might start to seek.

Secondly, AI can quickly start to enhance Business Agility and accelerate its progress and maturation. At a bare minimum, it will leave no option other than agile in IT as far as the development of AI solutions is concerned. This is because unlike some types of software development which can be quite standard, basically needing coding and plugging-in, model development process is by its very nature highly iterative, requiring multiple rounds of experimentation, performance evaluation and finetuning. There is a lot of creative problem-solving that goes into it.[23] Outside of IT, AI driven real time analytics will significantly enhance the sense and response capabilities of the organisation. In fact, corporations may even be able to adapt to market changes instantaneously harnessing predictive powers that have only been talked about in the science fiction domain so far. Innovation cycles will crash due to super-rapid prototyping and super-fast feedback cycles. AI assistants will augment the employees as short term contract workers who can be called upon at very short notice and this will make dynamic resource scaling a standard operating capability in agile organisations. Customer services will see a sea change as AI Bots take on the role of human service reps alongside humans and customers are not even able to distinguish between real human reps and AI Bot reps. All conversations could instantaneously be distilled and mined for opportunities to improve products and performance. Strategic agility will gain a new fillip because AI models will simulate innumerable scenarios at lighting speed using the latest real time market data. On the other hand, AI driven governance models will seek out and adapt to regulatory changes by suggesting new policies and procedures and implementing them within the regular work processes at speed and at scale. Security and compliance risks and issues will be monitored across channels and dealt with even before humans have had the chance to fully review or understand them. Through all of this, the limits of agility and adaptiveness will thereby scale new heights.

Finally, according to me, AI will accelerate the conversion and delivery of the real promise of Business Agility. It will allow us to be able to truly make the jump from today's narrowly defined 'value' in monetary terms of financial profit to a wider definition of 'value' which incorporates ethics, societal well being, and sustainable ecological benefits. The agile decision engine I have

---

[23] The Business Case For AI, Kavita Ganesan, Opinosis Analytics Publishing, 2022.

mentioned before would also be significantly fortified through AI to generate ethical implications for each decision choice resulting in decision processes that will have comprehensively considered all ethical dilemmas and ramifications. Perhaps a new era of caring capitalism will emerge.

PART V

JUST THE GOTCHAS

Not focusing on learning

"No one achieves perfection. But seeking it will motivate you to reject conventional wisdom in your search for newer, better methods and leadership practices. It also motivates you to develop continually as a human being" - Jean Dahl

Every Business Agility transformation journey is unique. While there are generically applicable lessons from organisations that have gone before, the reality is that there will be mistakes along the way. But with the right mindset and systems in place, these can be great opportunities to learn from. In fact, much of agility is about failing faster and therefore learning faster than the competition - in other words, it is about outlearning them. But unless a conscious effort is made to turn the organisation into a learning organisation, even experiments will be designed and conducted only to put up a show and simply comply with the guidance and requests from the Business Agility Office or senior leadership. This is also why building psychological safety is key. Without psychological safety in place, mistakes will lead to reprisals and stop the idea of learning and sharing right in its tracks. What is needed to build a learning culture is 'blameless postmortems' - not naming and shaming which unfortunately is still quite common to see, especially in large organisations. Structural and org design challenges leading to the buildup of information bottlenecks must be identified and removed as impediments to Business Agility. Skill concentration, key man dependencies, hero culture, communication technology related constraints, presence of unquestionable holy cows etc. are some of the issues that need to be watched out for and rooted out.

The good news is that people are intelligent and curious by design and crave learning to explore and excel. However, having worked in command-and-control based organisations where they were only required to follow orders, many unfortunately have learned not to question or experiment or take risks. Their natural curiosity has been dulled by only being allowed to learn what the company narrowly thinks is profitable for the business. Systems and controls have been built around this idea to keep staff from learning stuff that is not endorsed by management. It is as much of a mindset problem as it is a systems problem and often starts at the top. This mindset at the leadership level should be addressed on priority. Again, an accountability based coaching model will be very useful to help leaders make the transition. A common refrain in the book has been that for Business Agility to flourish, leadership must be ready and play its part wholeheartedly. The Business Agility Office and the CAO can play a very critical role in working with leadership teams, HR, and L&D departments to start and embed such a learning culture within the organisation as part of the agile transformation. Only then will 'Fail Fast and Learn Fast' become a reality rather than being an empty slogan or an aspired goal.

Assuming that such a mindset shift has indeed been achieved, it is a good idea to revisit the idea of Shu-Ha-Ri. Shuhari is a Japanese martial art concept which describes the stages of learning leading to mastery. Basically, if people are in the "Shu" (Follow) phase they are quite immature and they just follow the rules - in an enterprise context, this may sometimes mean simply adopting the team level practices of Scrum or Kanban by the book. If they are more mature, they will be in the "Ha" (Detach), where with new insights and understanding, they can break the rules safely. The last stage is the "Ri" (Transcend) phase where people are so mature that they can create their own rules. An example of focusing on learning based on the ShuHaRi principle might be the implementation of OKRs in the marketing function: initially they follow the OKR templates as closely as possible (Shu). In the Ha stage, they adapt OKRs to their specific campaigns using customised results. Ultimately, they transcend by developing innovative ways to continuously optimise their marketing strategies with or without industry standard OKR templates.

Not forming an Agile Executive Team

Forming an Agile Executive Team (AET) is a pivotal element in the journey of an organisation toward Business Agility. Comprising top-level executives and senior leaders, this team embodies agile principles and practices at the highest echelons of the company. The AET is indispensable for several reasons. Firstly, it sets the tone for agility across the entire organisation. By championing agile values, this team establishes a culture of adaptability and responsiveness. Secondly, it ensures alignment between strategy and execution, facilitating swift adaptation to changing market conditions. Lastly, it enables quicker decision-making and supports the removal of bureaucratic bottlenecks (a key factor that impedes agility as per the Business Agility equation mentioned at the beginning of the book). There are key differences between the AET and traditional executive teams:

Adaptability: AET embraces change and complexity. Traditional executive teams may be more resistant to departures from established norms.

Collaboration: Agile leadership is inherently collaborative. AET works as a collective leadership body, fostering a culture of teamwork and shared responsibility.

Empowerment: AET empowers teams and individuals, delegating authority and accountability. Traditional teams may encourage centralised decision-making.

Customer-Centric: AET prioritises customer value and feedback, ensuring that customer needs drive strategy. Traditional teams may be more internally focused.

Iterative Approach: AET operates iteratively, inspecting and adapting strategy and execution continuously. Traditional teams often adopt linear, plan-driven approaches.

The CEO and the Chief Agility Officer play a key role in forming this AET or in transforming a traditional executive team to an AET. It has been consistently done in virtually all organisations that have achieved enterprise-wide agility. A common mistake is to start and progress on the Business Agility journey without forming an AET. In those scenarios, Agile gets adopted in some functions or pockets but hit blockers that then remain as permanent blockers (often cultural and structural) and the promised benefits of Business Agility never really fructify because Business Agility forever remains out of reach - only a distant dream to be achieved someday. In other organisations, Business Agility came as an after-thought, after significant agile inroads were already made at an IT function level. But in many of these organisations, attempts were never made to form an Agile Executive Team. Regardless of how it came about, in such organisations the dream of Business Agility is eventually given up on and people that did adopt agile then leave slowly but surely.

Not focusing on Customer Delight

Doing agile without direct line of sight to the customer can be very counterproductive for developing Business Agility. The essence of Business Agility lies in staying closely connected to the customer, delivering value quickly without waste, and continuously adapting to her evolving needs and expectations (even leading her to satisfy her latent needs with newer innovative products and services). In other words, customer delight is the goal. Visualising her interactions and organising in an agile manner to deliver great service at every touchpoint is the way to get there.

A modern approach to visualise the customer's interactions and touchpoints with the organisation is to map them with 'customer journeys'. These are patterns of customer interactions each one leading up to a specific outcome for the customer. They are known as 'customer journey maps' and often built for specific 'customer personas'. Bits of critical information about customers are progressively and iteratively added and kept up to date in order to get full visibility into their needs, fears and frustrations across the chain of activities. This again requires active customer engagement and research and the concomitant investment to go into it. All functions, roles, and delivery constructs (teams, ARTs etc.) are then designed or redesigned to support these customer journeys and touchpoints in meaningful and impactful ways (even internal customer journeys can get created and are especially relevant for support functions like HR, Finance, etc. that primarily serve and support the organisation's employees rather than the end-customers).

While most organisations realise the importance of improving customer experience and some also increasingly feel the need to make their businesses agile, based on my personal experience, I see many of them fail to connect the two. As a result, they end up with good customer intentions that are not supported by their delivery organisation. They get a so-called agile organisation that can produce at pace but aren't able to move the needle when it comes to impact on the end-customers. Part of the problem is in the way that the agile transformation was started - did the challenge to be addressed and the vision for the transformation include the customer and the impact on her? Perhaps the transformation was only intended to reduce costs and improve speed to market? At other times, the root cause lies in the organisational model aspect - did the roadmap include adequate analysis and redesign of the operating model so that new practices would not be simply made to sit on a pre-existing disconnected model that has customer facing employees working at arm's length from product development or service delivery functions? Or, it could be that the agile workflows are working at the wrong level, targeting tasks and micro-work items that are too small to be able to deliver 'value' (i.e, scaling-up has not happened). Finally, it could be cultural and behavioural aspects - for example, do product managers actually go out and talk to customers or is that "simply not the way things work here" - perhaps only sales and marketing people talk to customers directly? Sometimes the customer's real needs and wants are just 'assumed' to be known and understood and this can turn out to be a big mistake - we all know the story of how Apple saw this and Nokia didn't, and the rest is history.

Starting a Business Agility journey only for the sake of Cost Reduction

"If you do not know how to ask the right question, you discover nothing" - *Eli Goldratt*

Many corporate transformations are done in order to get a cost advantage. A Business Agility journey will normally generate very significant cost savings, and this is well supported by research. In fact, maximising the amount of 'work not done' or in other words, maximising the amount of 'money not spent' is a key tenet of agile. However, it must be understood that these cost-savings will take time to materialise. In fact, such a journey will involve significant enterprise-wide investments initially.

Also, it must be understood that a significant portion of cost savings flow in indirectly through the reduction or avoidance of costs that may not even be currently counted by the existing accounting systems (a good practice that some organisations have started to implement is to utilise 'Lean Accounting' principles to capture the true costs being incurred [24]). Huge hidden costs start to become visible when you start to consider the cost of delays, cost of defects (quality), cost of carrying excess bureaucracy, and costs due to failure demand (also known as 'hidden factory' in Lean which refers to the invisible factory which exists just to repair stuff or make stuff no-one needs or produce stuff because there has been a failure upstream somewhere - this is equally if not more applicable in service scenarios where work itself is often invisible and in people's heads or inside computers!). Business Agility with its focus on transparency, inspection, and adaptation and the organisation-wide improvements that result from it makes these costs visible and easily targetable. For example, bad project investments can become apparent very quickly and be stopped or pivoted before significant costs accrue over months and years. Agile governance makes this possible. Also, cost performance keeps increasing consistently as teams continuously improve their technical excellence and ways of working with a keen focus on business results.

But Business Agility is much more than just about cost savings - as we have seen, it is so much about creating a healthy positive customer-centred culture and strong employee engagement. People feel energised, are empowered, and come to work together collaboratively in a focused and sustainable manner. The whole organisation gets driven by 'value' and this value is not just customer value and resultant economic value for the organisation but can also be expanded to include environmental and social value creation. You get to build an organisation that can pivot to become a sustainable business in the true sense of the word. Unlike traditional ways of running businesses, none of

---

[24] "Lean Accounting:Best Practices for Sustainable Integration" by Joe Stenzel, Catherine Stenzel, and Reza M. Pirasteh.

the agile principles are in conflict with the creation of such a sustainable business and a sustainable world. Robust ecological, social, and governance (ESG) practices is an increasingly important concern for most forward-thinking organisations today and Business Agility can positively impact the outcomes for each of these areas. Seeing Business Agility using a narrow lens (of cost reduction) will not enable the generation of all these potential benefits. In fact, a narrow focus on cost reduction can actually thwart the progress and spread of Business Agility. Such narrow focus on the golden swan instead of the golden eggs[25] will simply lead to a failed transformation effort with investments bigger than the realised benefits.

Drifting away from the Organisation's Strategy

"The main thing is to keep the main thing the main thing" - Stephen Covey

As we have seen before, for organisations mature in Business Agility, strategy is acknowledged to be both intentional as well as emergent. Since agility can sometimes narrowly be equated to autonomy, it is not impossible for the pendulum to swing too much and for the intentional element to be completely de-emphasised. Indeed, it is also possible for the enterprise to simultaneously focus on multiple emergent strategic issues and thereby lose the overall strategic coherence. Not making a choice at all or making too many conflicting choices can both lead to this state of zero coherence or in other words 'no strategy'. Organisations on the Business Agility journey should watch out for it.

---

[25] As per the story in Aesop's Fables, a farmer owns a goose that lays a golden egg every day. Instead of being patient, the farmer gets greedy and decides to cut open the goose, hoping to find all the golden eggs at once. However, he finds nothing, and the source of his wealth is lost. The fable teaches the lesson of not being too greedy and valuing long-term gains over short-term desires.

Case in point is an anonymous innovative tech company that had a core strategy of developing cutting-edge, high-priced, premium technology products that catered to a niche market. While autonomy, agility and emphasis on emergent strategies led to a surge in creative ideas, prototypes, and new initiatives, it also resulted in a significant shift in focus. Employees increasingly worked on low-cost, consumer-oriented products and features rather than the high-priced, premium products that had been the company's core intentional strategy. The company eventually struggled to maintain its premium brand image and lost some of its niche market due to these shifts.

What we really need is an approach that can perhaps be best described as 'aligned autonomy'. First, the organisation's overall strategy must be articulated, and it must be understood by everyone at any point in time. Unfortunately, it is all too common for teams to work out their own goals and direction of travel without a clear understanding of whereas an organisation they are all trying to go - the intentional strategy has not even been properly defined or communicated and hence no guiding framework for decision-making is available. Secondly, this intentional strategy must be cascaded in a way that every team and team of teams can understand what goals they must go after. Of course, with agility as the key operating principle, 'how' they go after the goals should be entirely down to them and not dictated down from the top. This is where the OKR (Objectives and Key Results) system that Google started comes in very handy and in fact, a lot of agile organisations have started utilising the concept successfully. OKRs are strategically utilised for changes and initiatives needed to go after the strategically important stuff, not the tactical or urgent BAU kind of work (for which KPIs and SLAs are still a good choice). OKRs can therefore help with enterprise-wide alignment to overall strategic themes and objectives that have already been defined. Thirdly, OKRs are defined and reviewed at short intervals based on results achieved (and feedback gathered) and the specific projects, initiatives, features and tasks are all decided by the individual teams or team of teams.

So, autonomy comes built into the framework. Finally, capital allocation, funding cycles and strategy reviews are made frequent and at shorter intervals. Existing initiatives and programs may get killed or new ones may get started at any point. This allows the emergent element of strategy to work its way through - this is how any significant changes are quickly sensed and responded to.

Not balancing Flexibility with Stability

The ability to strike a balance and be both flexible as well as stable is the hallmark of true Business Agility. While the agile movement has been a reaction to wide-spread ossification of processes and tools resulting in inflexibility and loss of value across industry sectors, equally there can indeed be such a thing as too much flexibility.

Once you succeed with agile, it is all too easy for teams to get too excited and start to apply agile methods even in places where they do not belong. Yes, it is possible for the pendulum to swing too far to one side and as a result, domains, processes and structures which need to be stable are now assumed to be part of the agile playground and up for grabs. In true agile spirit, experiments are conducted, and mistakes are made in places where learning new lessons (often in the form of reinventing the wheel) are costly and unnecessary. Cynefin framework comes with guidance here. It is a conceptual framework used to aid decision-making. Created in 1999 by Dave Snowden when he worked for IBM Global Services, it has been described as a "sense-making device" (Source- Wikipedia). Applying the framework helps us place ourselves in the right scenarios or "habitats," so that we can pair the right approach with our corresponding situation to achieve optimal outcomes. Cynefin consists of five domains: two of 'order' (the obvious and complicated), two of 'un-order' (complexity and chaos) and one of 'disorder' at the centre. In the 'obvious' domain there is no need for analysis - you simply sense, categorise, and respond as all it requires is following predefined rules and best practices. Waterfall can be a suitable approach in this domain. In the 'complicated' domain more judgement and analysis is required because although there are known unknowns, the problems and their solutions are knowable especially if experts are around. The best strategy here is to sense, analyse, and respond by selecting appropriate good practices and improving on them continuously towards perfection. Lean is a great fit for this domain. The next domain is called 'complex' and as the name implies, there are unknown unknowns and cause-effect relationships are difficult to establish. The best strategy is to probe, sense, and respond i.e. conduct experiments, understand the results, and implement the lessons learned. Naturally therefore, an agile approach is the best fit here. 'Chaotic' is often a transitory domain where there is too much instability, so time spent on learning is often wasteful as those learnings quickly become obsolete and pointless. The strategy here is to simply act fast to establish a degree of order, sense where some stability might exist, and respond by turning the chaotic into complex so that over time, stable patterns can be observed and understood. This is the territory of crisis management or firefighting and there are no repeatable learnings. Therefore, agile must not be applied everywhere willy nilly without first assessing whether it generates value. Otherwise, it can indeed be dangerous. Just as waterfall should not be the default approach when the situation is complex or complicated.

Within Business Agility theory and practice, there is definitely a place for stable elements. For example, while having multi-skilled teams is a core idea for Business Agility to thrive, it should not mean that the erstwhile functional anchors are gotten rid of completely. People still need a stable home where they can come to share specialised knowledge with other fellow experts and learn from each other. A successful approach to retain this advantage of the old pre-agile functional structures is to continue to have loosely held functional groups - they are now often called 'Communities of Practice' or 'Chapters' in some organisations. Good agile always makes space for stability and churn to co-exist.

Watch out for Fatigue and Burnout

"Faith is the bird that feels the light when the dawn is still dark" - Rabindranath Tagore

As we mentioned before, agile transformation should be done using an agile approach. Traditional big-bang transformations almost always lead to change fatigue and unfortunately an agile transformation done in that way is no different. Traditional organisation-change-management professionals (unless properly educated on Business Agility) also tend to deploy bureaucratic and process heavy change management approaches which can only make the journey feel worse. Actually, the road to Business Agility should be smooth and feel fun, enjoyable, and exciting if done correctly in an agile way. In my experience, people in general look forward to what they feel is a positive, achievable, and supported change. They actively participate with excitement and energy to make such changes stick. But three types of change efforts invariably run into fatigue and burnout issues - a) heavy handed transformations that teams are just expected to comply with b) the Transformation is focused mainly on cost cutting and productivity improvement with a tacit understanding and implication that more people will be let go and c) ones where teams started it bottom up but without any discernible shift in leadership behaviours or support from corporate level staff functions coming forth. These types of antipatterns are unfortunately all too common. According to Darren Faraway whom we have quoted earlier, a good example comes from Diageo - in one instance, a desire for more productivity led to a Programme Director using his authority to push for higher velocity (seen as a measure of productivity) from the agile teams. This led to teams gaming the measures by overestimating their work leading to increased velocity. Zero additional value was created because the actual output was still the same but only the measurement of it in terms of story points had artificially increased. (Fortunately, this anti-pattern skewed burn up the charts in Agile Reports which ultimately backfired). So, the lesson here is that traditional "push" and a narrow focus on productivity causes you more problems for no benefits in return.

A core principle of agile is embracing change and in fact, change management is actually an 'in-built' capability within agile teams. The Scrum Master, being the ground level steward of agile ways of working, should be close to every team member and be able to identify what is changing and react appropriately to early warning signs of fatigue in order to prevent team burnout. Sometimes, the time pressure of working in short time boxes (called Sprints under Scrum methodology) causes tensions in the short term and burnout over the longer term. But here again, the focus should be on reaching the Sprint goal (outcome) and not necessarily on every little output, user story (see Glossary) or task. Also, Scrum Masters play a critical role in protecting the team from unplanned work and interruptions during the Sprint and are expected to step in whenever conversations deflect away from being constructive to blame gaming. Re-emphasising the team's commitment to agile values and team agreement charter almost always helps. End of Sprint retrospectives (see Glossary) create yet another opportunity to really assess how a stressful trigger could have been prevented or managed better. Team happiness trends are also tracked by some teams and acted upon quickly. A good Scrum Master ensures that the team at all times is working at least on a few items that are purely meant to change processes, mental models, or behaviours rather than focusing on maintaining the status quo. In this respect, Business Change Management is continuously happening within teams and between teams in a self-managed manner.

The other thing to consider is pacing. Is the pace of change too fast for the people to absorb and sustain? While the vision and quarterly outcomes should flow top down, the exact ingredients of the changes and their timing should be owned by the teams at a pace that is sustainable for them. Too much, too soon, and driven from the top will only jeopardise the transformation - the journey is after all, a Marathon and not a Sprint (no pun intended). As mentioned before, it is better to carve out the change as a series of 'Transformation Sprints' with their own hypothesis, measures to test success, and 'in-built' ability to pivot whenever necessary. Similarly, too much collaboration in the name of agile can also lead to burnout and/or loss of productivity. Agile emphasises face to face interactions and customer collaboration and a huge array of modern-day tools are available to do this even virtually. But taken to an extreme, this can lead to too many meetings leading to meetings fatigue or what is now being reported in the popular business press as 'Zoom Fatigue'. This directly leads to wasted time which could have been utilised to do focused individual work or reflection. This is why it is important to continuously take the pulse of the people as they step into new ways of working. Leadership must engage actively and be present to interact and offer help with any issue or problem that the teams cannot solve for themselves. They should 'Go to the Gemba' (go visit the actual place of work) and collect direct feedback and qualitative data. Sometimes it is better to go slow on the transformation (at least initially) and take care of the cultural issues that invariably crop up before cranking up the speed (but still at a sustainable pace as every organisation has its natural speed limit set-point).

Stat: Manager burnout rose by 78% between Q1 and Q4 of 2020 according to the 2021 **State of the Manager report** from Glint and LinkedIn. Command and Control is not only ineffective but even more so and more stressful with distributed teams working through the Pandemic.

Author's Special Note: It is possible that teams are really fatigued because of traditional top-down change initiatives of the past. In such a context, even embracing agile can be seen as a top-down change - they just don't believe yet that all the good things being promised including the empowerment that comes with agile are real. I have found that involving customers and letting them provide the context and the need for change can work well in some such scenarios. Customer engagement and interaction is at the heart of agile in any case and realising the need for internal change because of the changes that the external customers expect from the organisation is sometimes enough to open eyes and create the initial momentum needed to get off the ground and start a new agile journey.

There will be Conflicts along the way

People have grown up in organisations thinking they belong to a certain job role in a certain function in a certain division and they have come to define themselves in terms of these narrow role based identities. With Business Agility, you become a different type of person - you go beyond your erstwhile narrow specialisation mindset to a cross functional mindset aligned to an end-to-end value stream. You begin to think of yourself as a T-shaped person i.e. while you continue to have specialised skills in an area, you also develop generalised knowledge and a broader skill set and connections. This change in identity and where one sees one's primary allegiance towards investing efforts and targeting goals can create tensions and conflict with others if not watched over and sensitively addressed by a mature and understanding leadership.

Also, agile teams will go through various stages of evolution before they become fully performing teams (see Tuckman's model[26]). After an initial period when they are very polite and accommodating of each other, the new ways of working create differences that must be addressed head-on, and conflicts arise. This is the storming phase. Conflict, defined as differences in opinions, perspectives, or viewpoints, is necessary for the success of any Agile team. But many Agile teams struggle to see conflict as healthy and disband or reconfigure before they're able to realise the benefits of working through the differences. Agile coaches must keep vigil and help the team surmount through the difficulties quickly and move on to the next phase.

---

[26] Tuckman, Bruce W (1965). "Developmental sequence in small groups". Psychological Bulletin.

As people become trained in agile and adopt new mindsets, they become much more acutely conscious of unhelpful as well as command-and-control behaviours. It is a fact that the whole enterprise will not switch on the Business Agility bulb in one go. In this interim period of transformation, conflicts are highly likely to arise between teams that have already adopted agile and those that are yet to. This is again a key watch-out scenario for the BAO who should work closely with Organisation Change, coaches, and leadership teams to mitigate and manage this.

Replacing Functional Silos with Product Silos

As we have discussed in the models of agile, it works best when teams (or teams of teams) are organised end-to-end as a value stream that cuts across functional silos. This leads to collaboration as everyone is aligned to a common product vision and objective. Often, these become fully product aligned teams and that is generally a good thing. However, as with all good ideas, there is always the danger that the idea is overdone and a religiosity and tribalism develops around it leading to almost exactly the same problem it was addressing in the first place - formation of closed boundaries and silos. When this happens, product teams become the new silos and stop collaborating with others forgetting that all product teams are ultimately serving the same organisation and its customers. Competition amongst products becomes the underlying dynamic. Cross-cutting organisational initiatives across product value streams are not given priority by anyone and it leads to an organisation with many agile teams but not much organisational agility.

Such a scenario can be prevented from being played out by emphasising from the very beginning on the importance of stewarding and growing a company-wide agile culture and 'being agile'. The top leadership teams play a critical role as we have mentioned before and equally the CAO and BAO are responsible to keep tabs on the pulse of the organisation continuously.

Running large cross-cutting Business Transformation projects in non-agile traditional manner

It is a big mistake to think that large projects that cut across different value streams or product aligned teams must run using traditional waterfall methods. It is true that large projects throw challenges and may not always fall neatly into classic agile territory. Often they need to work with hundreds of partially dedicated staff for example, the deliverables and scope is assumed to be known, and the time-scales are relatively fixed.

However, below the surface, many of the fixed elements are not really that fixed - this is the reason why even the construction industry (known to be operating in stable environments using standard benchmarks and practices) has adopted agile principles and practices. Understanding of the scope often varies initially, gradually becoming clearer over time—some aspects, even within regulation-driven projects, remain negotiable. Breaking down extensive work into smaller, incremental components (MVPs) proves valuable, allowing for iterative learning and the integration of feedback throughout the process.

A common backlog of work that everyone has visibility into, a way to add/remove work items freely without tight change controls, and a synchronised progression so that the various elements can come together at certain predefined points in time is not impossible to implement after all. What is needed is to identify the bureaucratic impediments that are blocking this from happening. Is it a set of bureaucratic procedures that need to be questioned and updated? Is it the reporting relationships and organisational construct that has been in existence to perfect the implementation of large projects over many years? Is it the mindset that says that we can't change because this is the only way that things can work here? An organisation and leadership that is maturing with agile will ask these questions and come up with the right balance of traditional and agile that works best - the answer will depend on the specific project context and the specific point in the overall maturity of the organisation in its journey towards Business Agility.

Another issue could be the traditional gap between business and IT that has not been addressed properly yet. Maybe the business is structured in a certain way to prioritise functional or siloed KPIs over cross-cutting initiatives. Maybe it's the incentive system that conflicts with the dedication and commitment required by everyone to make these horizontal initiatives successful. Or maybe it is again the attachment to the product view that we talked about in the previous 'Gotcha' to be wary of. A systems view must be taken to understand the big picture and the higher-level Business Agility impediments at work.

Not getting Middle Managers on the right side

Middle managers can make or break any agile transformation. In an agile transformation, middle managers are critical - to train, coach, mentor the team to real empowerment and success. They need to work with a 'relationship first' approach to enable collaboration and some organisations are indeed making it clear to them. Traditionally they have operated in an environment where building close relationships with their 'subordinates' was seen as being risky. Productivity of everyone under their command was the key metric for them to chase and protect. Being friendly was almost taboo since that would often be perceived as 'being too nice' and detrimental to squeezing the maximum productivity out of the employees. So the new behaviours expected from Business Agility champions is indeed countercultural and can feel quite radical to them.

Managers also feel insecure as they are now left in the middle with opposing sets of expectations. On the one hand they are still being made accountable for results but on the other hand they are not 'in charge' to command and control their teams - they can't 'tell' them anymore what to do and how to do it. Similarly, the emphasis shifts from a traditional highly visible 'command and control' crisis management mode to a servant leadership based 'crisis prevention' mode (which seems much less visible and demonstrable to higher ups and bosses who used to hold the powers on individual rewards and promotions). Therefore, the shift from command and control to servant leadership seems like an insurmountable obstacle and unless this fear and insecurity is addressed with empathy, middle managers can become the biggest saboteurs of Business Agility. What then results is a lot of doing agile and going through the motions half-heartedly without really achieving the benefits that result from true agile transformation. Added to this is the fact that managers in many organisations have learnt over time that the so called 'transformations' merely come and go just as senior leaders and CEOs come and go. They have seen that priorities almost always shift as new leaders replace old ones and hence they reason that what really matters is simply riding out this new wave of 'agile transformation' only until the next CIO or CEO comes in and hopefully resets the organisational trajectory and approach.

Obviously these entrenched mindsets and beliefs need changing if Business Agility is to become a reality. This is where enterprise leadership, the Business Agility Office (BAO), and Business Change professionals (typically with HR backgrounds) should play an important role. Behaviour generally falls into repetitive patterns and the automaticity is not easy to break without external help. So, each individual middle manager must be supported through the change with customised services, mentoring, and coaching. Experienced agile coaches are trained to see the negative behavioural loops that are going on and are able to inject interventions along specific points on those cycles so that the habitual thoughts and the resultant emotions and behaviours can change. Sometimes this coaching may also involve transitioning some of the managers to new and/or redefined roles as few (if any at all) command and control roles will continue to be required. But, the key point is while it is true that a mature agile organisation will not need as many middle managers as it needed in the past, there will still be a strong demand for these experienced employees to take up redefined and / or new roles as people managers or guild/ 'community of practice' leaders.

Watch out for Agile Extremism

As we have seen, there are many agile frameworks that are available and have been successfully implemented. Scrum happens to be one such very popular framework but by no means the only one. Each has its merits, advantages and weaknesses and it really depends on the type of organisation you are (for example you could be a software product company or a battery manufacturer or a large MNC bank or a hospital), the size, the domain being considered etc. Basically, it is context dependent. For example, while scrum or XP works great for a software development team, when it comes to scaling-up or scaling-out, these are not necessarily the best ones to use although one can go a certain way with methods utilising scrum of scrums or scrum of scrum of scrums. Popular frameworks like SAFe, LeSS, DSDM, DAD, unFIX, FlightLevels and others can be considered instead for best applicability at a scaled level. Agile extremism arises when people get wedded to a particular method and try to apply it everywhere as 'the' silver bullet just because one is trained/experienced with it or have applied it successfully in one corner of the enterprise. For enterprise Business Agility in an organisation above a certain size, it is often the case that multiple frameworks are applied in different areas and there is nothing wrong in that necessarily. Also, it can be a good idea to blend and mix the best of breed and evolve practices empirically based on what works. While there is theory and guidance available in most frameworks, 'empiricism' is a huge thing for achieving Business Agility. Ironically though, in this you will need guidance from unbiased and pragmatic agile coaches (rather than from those that dogmatically follow agile methods like a religion). It must never be forgotten that in agile, nothing is to be considered as 'best practice' or immutable - we are always uncovering better ways to work and that holds true for frameworks or the plethora of practices recommended in them. It is also known as 'double loop learning' wherein you question 'what' you are doing and adapt rather than simply change the 'how' of what you are doing.

Also, it is important not to ignore ancillary approaches (these include Design Thinking, Lean Start-Up, DevOps, etc.) to work together with the pure agile approaches and processes that originated in software development. Lean and Kanban practices can be readily wrapped around most agile practices to provide maximum benefit. They can be utilised even on their own in some contexts. Business Agility unlike 'agile within IT' is a larger set and inclusive of other complementary methods and practices that can work together to make the enterprise more adaptive and resilient at scale. Having a biassed view towards one or a few over others is not helpful and should be avoided.

Finally, as we have pointed out earlier, Business Agility can still flourish whilst having agile practices and traditional waterfall practices peacefully coexist (although it must be said that the argument for continuing with waterfall approaches will become less and less tenable in the future). Trying to root out traditional management practices altogether from everywhere in the enterprise in the name of agile is just another form of agile extremism.

No time or space for Innovation

"If I had asked my customers what they wanted, they would have said a faster horse"- Henry Ford, when talking about the adoption of his motor car

Agile teams by definition are mostly working on innovation problems. As we have mentioned before, where the environment is fixed and demand (scope of work) is predictable, stability is the key requirement and traditional approaches can work perfectly fine. There is little need for learning in such situations. Most work however has components with inherent variability and uncertainty. This is where the best answers are yet unknown and therefore demands innovation. The process involves creative visualisation of what might work, experimentation to let it play out in reality, inspection and reflection, and finally adaptation to implement the innovation before another cycle begins once again. But this can happen only if agile teams get the right support and slack time. Often, they get neither. In my experience, this is because it is seen as an expense rather than an investment. Without an agile mindset shift, managers will continue to exhibit 'innovator's dilemma'[27] and will try to prioritise existing products, processes, practices and well understood standard features over changed or newer practices unwittingly if not wilfully.

"Google employees are encouraged to spend 20% of their time working on new projects and improving their performance by researching and developing new ideas" - Google Founders' IPO letter. Being an agile organisation operating at the forefront of innovation, Google understands that true innovation can only get sparked when employees are empowered and trusted to freely spend their 'innovation time' as they want - there is no corporate restriction or guidance on what they can work on. This is how products like Google Adsense, Gmail, Google News were all born. This underscores how much leadership's trust in employees and willingness to forego immediate productivity can result in ultimately market-winning products and performance. This is also the reason behind the increasingly popular 'Freedom Fridays' for example. SAFe, a well -regarded scaled agile framework emphasises one iteration (say 2 weeks) of 'innovation and planning' for every 'Programme Increment' (typically 10-12 weeks) of work.

---

[27] The Innovator's Dilemma - The innovator's dilemma: Christensen, C. M. (1997) When new technologies cause great firms to fail. Harvard Business School Press.

Idea recognition, idea generation, idea selection, concept development and concept testing all benefit greatly from well entrenched lean agile practices like Design Thinking, Hackathon/Make-a-thon, Lean Start-Up etc. Similarly, principles of 'Jugaad' (an Indian word roughly meaning the use of skill and imagination to find an easy, inexpensive solution to a problem) or 'frugal innovation' are very compatible with agile principles and are a great fit for agile teams to apply and do great work when it comes to innovation.

Another way to spark innovation is for leaders to allow the reduction and elimination of context switching. Agile teams are designed to avoid context switching by always staying focused in their work through to completion. Context switching is a huge productivity and creativity killer when it comes to innovative work. A scientist named Harold Pashler demonstrated this in the early 1990's. He called it "Dual Task Interference." Pashler theorised that there was some sort of processing bottleneck happening in a person's brain when multitasking. That people can really only think about one thing at a time, that a certain amount of effort was involved in packing up one process, reaching into your memory and pulling out another, and then running that job. And each time you switch tasks, that process takes extra effort and time. Numerous other studies show the same thing. Without an agile mindset shift, organisations still narrowly focus on resource productivity and operate under the notion that multitasking is good. As a result, time and space is not provided for innovation to flourish.

Teams also need the right kind of collaborative work-spaces (and the right remote working tools) that have been shown to increase creative output by manifolds. Being physically or virtually close to each other matters a lot because more than individual talent and creative ideation, it is the connection and bouncing of ideas and a joint play-like dynamic that fosters real innovation. In other words, teams need to be able to work collaboratively. This won't happen if the Facilities department is solely incentivised to optimise cost per square foot for example. Of course, communication is the key denominator in all this and the critical factor when it comes to knowledge and creative work - as per work done by Tom Allen from MIT, communications fall off extremely steeply with distance between team members (e.g. probability of communicating at least once weekly is about 30% when distance is within 2 metres but reduces to 5% when it is 5 metres and continues to decrease with every added metre)[28].

When it comes to innovation, Hexagon Manufacturing Intelligence, part of Hexagon AB group, is one of the companies that helps develop the disruptive technologies of today (cloud, robotics, sensors, digital twins, AI) and life changing products of tomorrow – ensuring a scalable, sustainable future. Hexagon has more than 24,000 employees across 50 countries and a market cap of 35 B USD. Hexagon is not a startup. But like any large enterprise company today, it values agility. It strives to build agility into the DNA of the company. In the past few years, Hexagon has invested and made significant inroads in its business agility journey. For Hexagon, making time and space for innovation is crucial to being agile. According to Parth Joshi, Chief Product and Technology Officer of Hexagon Manufacturing Intelligence, based in Atlanta, Georgia, a key aspect is to look at innovation from the point of view of two portfolios - one is the continuous innovation on the stable foundation for the current products. The second is the disruptive and growth-oriented innovation portfolio. Particularly on the disruptive portfolio, Hexagon focuses on bringing to bear the agile values, principles, and practices - customer feedback, failing fast, retrospectives, and incremental funding based on market vetting, etc. This also has necessitated working collaboratively with external startup organisations in a mutually beneficial way and requires an agile approach to drive mutual success. Internally, Hexagon actively promotes hackathons, innovation days, and accelerator programs and ensures funding is tied to the results and outcomes generated. One of the key lessons learned at this company is to let agile principles of

---

[28] Thomas J. Allen, Managing the Flow of Technology (Cambridge, MA: MIT Press).

passion, self-initiative, and self-organisation take root. People with ideas and passion, regardless of place in the hierarchy, self-initiate project experiments and self-select team members, while agile coaches and managers maintain oversight of the results and jointly decide how to scale.

Author's Special Note: Organisations that have taken innovation and learning seriously have gone ahead and encouraged employees and teams to go out and do collaborative work outside of company borders. Participation in external meetups, open-source innovation projects, and learning labs is encouraged because for true innovation to spark on, external stimuli and absorption of learning generated outside of organisational boundaries is important. Also, when external consultants are hired, they are contractually expected to pass on knowledge and help embed better ways of working rather than paid to simply provide advice and leave. On the other hand, innovation laggards often struggle with the 'not invented here' syndrome and shut out all external ideas and inputs - the dominant belief is 'we know best and what works elsewhere won't work here' - a very anti-agile 'fixed' mindset. A common tired refrain heard often is 'we are different - our industry is different; our company is different'.

Not changing the Performance Management System

"Without fear, we will see many more problems, mistakes, and opportunities for improvement" - W. Edwards Deming

Business agility can thrive only when there is transparency. However, it is to be understood in its correct interpretation with regard to agility. Transparency is key because it is the precursor to the 'inspect and adapt' idea behind lean and agile. Teams take accountability and responsibility for continuous learning and improvement and truly start to deliver only when the right data is collected and made available to them. Based on this data, teams (or team of teams) should be able to spot problems beforehand or at least as soon as they occur. They should also be able to reflect at regular intervals and at multiple levels based on evidence and trends. As a single entity accountable for a particular customer outcome, they should be able to adapt and observe the effects of any experiment they conduct (i.e. a changed process or way of working for example) first hand and as quickly as possible. But all this falls apart when transparency is done merely for the sake of management to get an inside view of all the details. Of course, they then barge in, try to solve problems, and micro-manage. There is always a case for management and leadership to be equipped with the right data so that higher level decisions can be made through lean governance processes. But that data is aggregated data only and designed as needed. The team members need to have a certain level of privacy and empowerment in terms of what data they collect, analyse, and how they run their shop as a 'self-organised team' (see Glossary).This is what creates an environment for teams to actually use numbers for improvement rather than numbers to game - an untoward situation all too common in most traditionally run enterprises. The metrics are to be seen as enablers of agility rather than as performance targets to be met (somehow and anyhow!) out of fear of reprimands, criticism or missing out on rewards. Driving out fear from the workplace is a fundamental requirement for building Business Agility. This was foreseen and strongly advocated by pioneers of modern non-traditional (aka non Tayloristic) management methods - especially people like Edward Deming, who initiated the TQM movement and helped hasten Japan's recovery after the second world war in the 1950s and beyond. His philosophy emphases the avoidance of blame and encourages the redefinition of mistakes as opportunities for improvement.

The other gotcha when it comes to performance management systems for Business Agility is to continue to have individual driven appraisal systems. For Business Agility, we want to move away from a harshly individualistic and competitive way of working to team-based success definitions. Individuals achieve success together as part of being on a high performance agile team.

Teams help their newer or weaker members to rapidly learn and contribute to team success. In fact, once cross-functional empowered teams are given the purpose, agreed success criteria, and a conducive supportive environment, they quickly evolve to become high performance self-managed teams and do not tolerate low performing individuals that are still somehow not able or willing to learn and develop. Such self-control mechanisms are inbuilt within agile teams and emerge quite quickly during or after transition to agile ways of working. This has been seen to be the case in almost all good agile transformations. Consequently, the number of high performing individuals increases significantly in the organisation. The way this happens is because with an agile mindset and ways of working, people start to really focus (immediate goals that are aligned with long term purpose and vision), learn to collaborate to achieve more, use their autonomy to think laterally and solve problems creatively, make steadfast commitments, and learn at pace. But again, despite more numbers of high achievers, for this to work, the key requirement is to replace individual performance based scoring and reward systems with one that is based on team performance and shared rewards. The logic is that as teams become high-performing (and individuals perform better too), the team receives greater rewards (which also means that ultimately individuals get better rewards). It is illogical to think that people in teams will collaborate with each other and with other teams and stakeholders in full measure when the performance system still rewards the exact opposite - competition and individual success. Having mentioned all the above, it is also true that a few individuals initially struggle with the new system - they feel lost and unseen and are worried that their strong contributions and performance will now get hidden behind the veil of team success. There is definitely a coaching and people change management angle here and HR will need to keep a close line of sight during the transition.

Not modernising the Legacy IT estate

"The greatest danger in times of turbulence is not the turbulence itself, but to act with yesterday's logic." - Peter Drucker

This directly impacts Business Agility as it relates to technical debt accumulation which is a key factor in the Business Agility equation introduced at the beginning chapter of the book. Many organisations are still having to tolerate very old legacy technology applications that are still core to their operations and business. Often there are multiple such applications or platforms that the organisation is relying on and these are so old that the code is nothing less than a spaghetti - very difficult to maintain and almost impossible to support modern development needs. A patchwork of middleware and connections are then built on top of these legacy applications to ensure that single views of information are possible. It introduces big risks as it is difficult to run comprehensive tests for any change being introduced. While Refactoring (an agile technical practice from XP framework) needs to be done regularly on such systems just to keep them running, all this slows down services and limits the IT department's ability to be responsive to the business. Also, many more people are needed to run the IT function meaning less money and resources are available to invest in chasing new customers and discovering new value. This is how a problem that is thought to be localised in the technology architecture area makes the whole enterprise inflexible and slow.

Business and IT are not separate anymore in today's digital world and a problem in IT means a problem for the whole business. These problems mean foregoing money-making opportunities (opportunity loss) and also risk of sudden unplanned expenditures on incident management and damage control. Postponing investments in modernising technology and in writing clean code will not help. There is therefore a key lesson in all this. While the cost of modernisation can be high, it is unfortunately a price that needs to be paid either directly in order to move to a simpler IT landscape or by continuing to pay the increasingly high hidden costs of being slow and unsafe. The more separated IT and business are in an enterprise, the less appreciation there is of the need to invest in modern technology - a commitment to Business Agility forces these conversations to happen if done the right way.

Relying exclusively on technical Agile coaches and consultants for Business Agility transformation

Most agile coaches today have earned their stripes in IT. This is not a bad thing and to be expected because as you know very well by now, the agile movement was born in software development and most of the adoption has largely been in IT only. So agile coaches generally have a very good understanding of designing and accelerating agile adoption in the technology function. To some extent they also know how to coach businesspeople to become more effective at product ownership or business stakeholders to better support product development by having them to share business context, objectives etc with development teams. Business Agility changes all that because while many of the skills are directly transferable, a real appreciation of business context and the pressures and challenges that are faced in non-tech areas is often missing amongst many of these coaches. Most have not spoken the language of business or have not extensively worked with business executives. Many have not had any exposure to approaches like Lean as it applies to business operations for example. Nor have they ever tried to address continuous business improvement challenges, sales/marketing issues or radical step changes with quantitative problem-solving approaches like six sigma. Do they really understand the nuances and interrelationships between the plethora of capabilities and the supporting processes within functions like HR or Finance? Simply retrofitting a scrum process on all the people in HR or first requiring them to be all part of teams (even if they can only be partially dedicated to these because most of the work is functional tasks) for example will not solve any problem or yield any benefit of agile. Basically, it is easy to miss important pieces of the ecosystem or overlook important details when designing transformation for an end-to-end slice of the enterprise. Nuances can be easily missed by those who only know IT, the way software development processes work, and what improvement and collaboration means within the boundaries of that technology context. This is one of the key reasons why so many agile transformation coaches have shied away from taking an end-to-end scope or running real Transformation Sprints outside of the technology function. After all, even agile coaches like any other human being are psychologically wired to prefer comfort zones too.

The solution lies in ensuring that the organisation invests in the Chief Agility Officer and the Business Agility Office mentioned earlier. This office, in collaboration with HR and the business PMOs recruit the right kind of talent (both internally and externally) and form right skilled teams to start and sustain Business Agility transformations. Having generalist skills across business and tech with deep skills in a few specific areas of agile become critical. In my experience, some senior business analysts, functional staff, and business architecture experts who have significant experience with agile and other improvement approaches can sometimes fit these roles very well. They can then work collaboratively with technical agile coaches (which the organisation would already usually have) and bring everyone up to speed over time. This diversity of experience and skillset can make or break Business Agility journeys. The availability of such multi-spectrum skills and exposure is unfortunately still quite limited in the market as most coaches today hail from the technology domain but over time this is expected to increase as more and more enterprises undertake their front-to-back Business Agility transformations.

PART VI

THE SCIENCE BEHIND BUSINESS AGILITY

"He who loves practice without theory is like the sailor who boards ship without a rudder and a compass- and never knows where he may cast" - *Leonardo da Vinci*

Business agility is grounded in empiricism. This implies that most of what is propounded or accepted as 'what works' is based on lessons learned from conducting experiments and direct observation. And because it is so, every organisation while staying true to the basic principles and values must evolve the shape of the journey and the particular practices on their own based on the experiments they conduct and lessons they learn along the way. Speed of learning is thus of much more significance than of copying so called 'best-practices'. This is often known as 'fail-fast' in agile circles.

However, mentioned below are some of the underlying theories and concepts that have been used in agile organisations to ensure that their experiments are based on solid research and scientific footing.

Metcalf's Law

Metcalf's Law states that the value of a system grows at approximately the square of the number of users of the system, meaning the more the people are using it, the more their participation enhances the network. This therefore explains why telecom networks in general and the Internet in particular have become so powerful. From a Business Agility perspective, it relates back to teams and their sizes. It explains why agile teams must be small teams because with each additional member, there are 'n' new connections that need to be established for trust to get created and performance to result. Also, smaller teams prevent a phenomenon called 'social loafing' which saps team engagement and efficiency over the long term. All of this requires work to be broken down into smaller chunks that are consumable by small teams. The other dark side of Metcalf's Law is that unless understood and actively watched out for, let loose, it will lead to too many emails, too many meetings and communication related burnout. As per Bain & Company, as much as 30% productivity loss is happening due to this lack of engagement and time-waste.

Dunbar's number

First proposed by British anthropologist Robin Dunbar, it is a theoretical cognitive limit to the number of people with whom one can maintain stable social relationships. By using the average human brain size and extrapolating from the results of primates, he proposed that humans can comfortably maintain 150 stable relationships. From an agile perspective, when we consider Agile Release Trains or tribes or many people cooperating in some way, the ability to maintain trust and personal relationships is key to creating teams of teams.

Pareto Principle

Named after Italian economist Vilfredo Pareto, who noted the 80/20 connection saying approximately 80% of the land in Italy was owned by 20% of the population. Mathematically, it is also known as the power law and holds true in most natural and social phenomena. Based on this, we look for the 20%

of customers who represent 80% of the needs or 20% of the features (backlog prioritisation) that satisfy 80% of the customers when we build agile solutions. Also, we focus on the 20% of issues from a retrospective that will resolve 80% of the problems. Scarce resources like agile coaches can also be allocated selectively to 20% of the teams that need them most or produce 80% of the results impacting overall objectives. Can be directly related to the 10th Agile Principle: "Simplify: maximise the amount of work not done" (to know all the agile principles, check the section Agile vs Agility in part I of this book)

Ashby's Law of Requisite Variety

W. Ross Ashby was a British cyberneticist and psychologist who, during the 1960s, proposed a law with regards to levels of variety and regulation within biological systems, i.e. variety absorbs variety. In his words: "When the variety or complexity of the environment exceeds the capacity of a system (natural or artificial) the environment will dominate and ultimately destroy that system". For example, in a Sports match, the winning team may attack with more variety than the losing team is capable of defending (as they may have not practised with as much repertoire of variety). The more variable the operational environment, the more flexible the organisation and its internal systems need to be in order to respond adequately and survive. This lies at the heart of the agile concept.

Amara's Law

Named after Roy Amara (1925–2007), the Law states - "We tend to overestimate the effect of a technology in the short run and underestimate the effect in the long run." All too often organisations turn to tools, technologies, and practices for answers without taking into account the cost of adoption, cost of ownership, and strategic ramifications. Often the immediate results are therefore less than anticipated but if persisted with then over time the amplification effects of combining different elements and practices of agile build up exponentially. Very relevant for understanding large transformations and for change management.

Little's Law

An MIT professor named John Little developed this theorem we call Little's Law. It states that "the average number of items within a system is equal to the average exit rate of items out of the system multiplied by the average amount of time an item spends in the system". It is mathematically expressed as WIP = Throughput X Lead Time; where WIP is work-in-progress.

The fundamental result of Little's Law is that for a given process, in general, the more things that you work on at any given time (on average) the longer it is going to take for each of those things to finish (on average). As a case in point, managers who are ignorant of this law panic when they see that their Cycle Times are too long and perform the exact opposite intervention of what they should do: they start more work. After all, they reason, if things take so long, then they need to start new items as soon as possible so that those items finish on time—regardless of what is currently in progress. (Source: Daniel Vacanti, https://www.scrum.org/resources/littles-law-professional-scrum-kanban#:~:text=The%20fundamental%20result%20of%20Little's,to%20finish%20(on%20average).

Multitasking Law

Contrary to accepted wisdom, just because people and particularly managers multitask all the time does not mean that it is the best way to finish work. A principle of Lean is "flow" (i.e. continuous flow of work items without stoppage or interruptions along the way) and one of the ways to make flow happen is to focus on "start finishing and stop starting". In other words, no multitasking! Multitasking is actually a symptom and coping mechanism to deal with a bad system in which decision or wait times far exceed the task times. It has been proven through multiple studies as well as empirically that multitasking leads to lower throughput, lower productivity, and lower efficiency due to longer lead times (all due to a costly brain phenomenon called "context switching"). As per research conducted by Gerry Weinberg[29], loss of working time due to context switching goes up from 0% (if focused on only one project) to as much as 40% (if working on 3 projects) to 75% (if working on 5). This is obviously a huge loss of productivity but unseen, unrecognised and accepted in traditional, non-agile systems of work. Multitasking, despite best intentions to maximise utilisation of resources and skilled people, reliably reduces flow.

The lean agile solution is to go to the root and prevent the need for multitasking. This is done either by eliminating dependencies (say by forming cross functional teams) and/or by creating specific policies like work in process (WIP) limits. If we break work into small pieces and only work on one thing at a time per person, we can optimise our ability to get things done.

Conway's Law

Mel Conway first postulated his thesis and stated that "Any organisation that designs a system (defined broadly) will produce a design whose structure is a copy of the organisation's communication structure." In other words, If two teams are building a part of a solution separately, that solution will probably have two components, introducing dependencies and additional communication load. The solution in agile to this problem is to first break down the silos that will constrain teams to produce a holistic customer need focused solution. Small, cross-functional co-located (physically or virtually) teams have therefore been a cornerstone of all popular agile frameworks.

---

[29] Weinberg, Gerald M, Quality Software Management – Volume 1: Systems Thinking

Knowledge Worker Motivation

Dan Pink's work on knowledge worker productivity is a key study that supports agile work design. In his book "Drive", he explains that the three factors that are most critical for knowledge worker productivity are a) Purpose, b) Autonomy and c) Mastery. With most complex work being knowledge work, Business Agility cannot flourish unless people feel a visceral connection with a larger goal or mission beyond their immediate day to day. I.e. the work needs to matter to them. They also need autonomy to make decisions regarding the work as they know their job best and are often closest to the customer. And knowledge workers flourish when there is opportunity to practise, learn, and develop their craft to the next level. All these are intrinsic motivators that must be present for agile ways of working to take root and mature. Mere monetary rewards will never nearly be enough.

Thinking fast and slow

This is a seminal book and author Daniel Kahnemann explores in detail the two systems of thinking that drive human decision. System 1 is fast and intuitive thinking whereas System 2 is our slow and deliberate thinking. A successful journey to Business agility requires deliberate System2 thinking and reflection because a significant portion of agile thinking and practice challenges traditional set norms established in the workplace over many decades and centuries. Kahnemann also talks about various biases that humans routinely fall into, and it will be useful to consider these when undertaking agile transformations. Loss aversion is another critical concept introduced in the book. Traditionally, organisations may have sidestepped small batches of work and interactive sessions (agile ceremonies for example) equating them with an increase in wasted time. These could be 'reframed' so that people in organisations realise that actually there is a bigger loss to be experienced unless newer and nimbler approaches are adopted - this can help usher in a 'growth mindset' in the enterprise if the psychological science contained in the book is properly applied by agile coaches and leaders.

Complex Adaptive Systems

The term complex adaptive system was coined in 1968 by sociologist Walter F. Buckley who proposed a model of cultural evolution which regards psychological and socio-cultural systems as analogous with biological species. In "An Introduction to Society as a Complex Adaptive System" Buckley explores the idea of society as a complex adaptive system. In the book, Buckley discusses how social systems, like biological systems, exhibit emergent properties and self-organising behaviours. Unlike a system governed by a propensity to return to equilibrium after being disturbed, and in doing so losing structure as entropy increased, Buckley's Complex Adaptive Systems built up structure as they adapted against new external and internal interactions. He introduces concepts like complexity of social systems, feedback loops, information processing, network thinking and adaptation, highlighting how these elements shape the dynamics of society.

Buckley's work is thus significant in the context of designing and optimising modern organisations, especially in the realm of agile ways of working. It provides a theoretical foundation for understanding the dynamics of complex social systems and offers insights into the principles that are essential in agile organisations. It encourages a holistic and flexible approach to organisational design, aligning with the agile philosophy of adaptability and responsiveness.

Ikea Effect

The Ikea effect basically states that we place higher value on things we partially created ourselves - e.g. - "Don't you love this room; I designed the decor and painted the walls myself" or I built and installed the furniture myself using the flatpack from Ikea! Business agility requires motivated teams and one of the key things for people to take pride in their work is to have the empowerment to design and deliver it themselves. Most agile practices like Planning, Stand-ups, Confidence Voting, Innovation Time etc. are there because they directly create this empowerment.

Westrum Typology and Information Flow

Ron Westrum's research on information flow is closely tied to organisational culture and safety. He's known for his work on the "Westrum typology," which classifies organisational cultures into three categories based on the flow of information: Pathological, Bureaucratic, and Generative.

A) Pathological Culture: In this culture, information is hoarded and often used as a source of power. Employees are afraid to report problems or mistakes due to fear of punishment. This culture is detrimental to safety, as critical information is suppressed, leading to potential hazards going unaddressed. B) Bureaucratic Culture: Bureaucratic cultures have formal procedures, but information flow is selective and controlled. There's a focus on compliance with rules and regulations. Safety is a concern and managed, but incidents may still occur due to information bottlenecks and slow response times. C) Generative Culture: Generative cultures encourage open and honest communication. Information flows freely, and there's a proactive approach to learning from mistakes. Safety is a top priority, and incidents are less likely to occur. When they do, they are thoroughly investigated to prevent recurrence.

Safety is a key feature of organisations that have reached maturity on Business Agility. Westrum's work underscores the critical link between an organisation's culture, its approach to information flow, and its safety performance.

PART VII

CHECKLISTS, TEMPLATES & GLOSSARY

Leader's Alignment Checklist

The Mirror Test

This checklist will help you see how aligned you naturally are to agile values and principles: Answer in Yes or No

1. Management that is destructively critical when mistakes are made kills initiative

2. As our business grows, it becomes increasingly necessary to delegate responsibility and to encourage men and women to exercise their initiative

3. Control is more important than Autonomy as Compliance is more important than Engagement

4. Developing a learning culture is important and for learning cultures to develop, it doesn't matter what people learn

5. To stay competitive and boost innovation, we must become very good at frequently reallocating people to new opportunities

6. As a good leader people want me to be strongly decisive

7. I expect my team members to be smart and therefore quickly get my idea and vision for any new initiative

8. As a good leader I expect myself to follow through on decisions and ensure everyone is sticking to plans and agreed milestones

9. It is easy to see the linear cause effect relationships and physics that exist in any organisation but challenging to change because people naturally resist change

10. As a senior leader I have too little time and too much at stake to be able to really commit to or track my own personal learning and development

11. I don't feel satisfied unless I see everyone attending a meeting speak up and express their true opinions and ideas

12. It is a good idea as a senior leader to join the teams' daily meetings (sometimes) to check that the aggregated RAG reports being presented at senior levels do indeed reflect the status on the ground

13. I believe that the number of errors generated by a team is a good measure of their effectiveness because good teams generate fewer defects

14. I truly believe that 'Perfection is the enemy of Good'

15. In a meeting, I like to express my views first as it sets the tone and makes the meeting more efficient

List of Corporate Values to emphasise Agility

It may be useful to review your organisation's current set of stated values and compare them with those listed below. Values drive behaviours and become the culture - 'the way things get done'. Certain values cultivate Business Agility while others may interfere. But even the right values must be lived within the boundaries set by the organisation's context. Most of these recommended values below have been mentioned and extensively talked about throughout the book in various sections.

1. **Customer Value:** Being focussed on discovering and delivering value to customers quicker than competitors (or at least quicker than before)

2. **Experimentation:** Being empowered to take risks, experiment, and learn from failure and successes

3. **Swift adaptation:** Being swiftly adaptable and responsive to changing environments and market needs

4. **Collaboration:** Being collaborative within a team, across teams and with customers/suppliers

5. **Accountability:** Being accountable for performance and success in the market

6. **Digitally enabled:** Being enabled by digital technologies and automation to reduce friction

7. **Data driven:** Being decisive and measurement oriented using data as the key input

8. **Scaled-down:** Being an admirer of small batches of work to be started and finished within short timeboxes by relatively small teams

9. **Responsible citizenship:** Being responsible especially with respect to privacy, social and environmental impact

10. **Openness:** Being transparent and open with respect to communication

11. **Simplicity:** Being always on the lookout to make strategies, systems, and structures simpler and easier to navigate for customers, staff and partners

12. **Security and Safety:** Being protective and safety focussed

13. **Respect:** Being respectful of others and their uniqueness as human beings

14. **Happiness:** Being empathetic to an employee's need for finding meaning and happiness at work. Autonomy, purpose and mastery are key here.

15. **Lateral leadership:** Being flexible with leadership roles and responsibilities

ANSWERS TO THE MIRROR TEST

The correct answers are given below but you are encouraged to visit www.businessagility.org for getting a score and a deeper understanding of the responses. You may also purchase more copies of the book and gain other valuable insights from the website.

1. Yes
2. Yes
3. No
4. Yes
5. No
6. No
7. No
8. No
9. No
10. No
11. Yes
12. No
13. No
14. Yes
15. No

GLOSSARY

- Agile Release Train: An ART is a long-lived team of agile teams that incrementally develops, delivers, and often operates one or more solutions in a value stream

- Centre of Excellence (CoE): A centre of excellence (CoE) is a team of skilled knowledge workers whose mission is to provide the organisation they work for with best practices around a particular area of interest

- Leading/Lagging Indicators: Leading indicators are predictive and indicative of events before they happen and are therefore process and input oriented measures. Lagging indicators are output oriented and measured after an event has occurred.

- Minimum Viable Product: A version of a new product which allows a team to collect the maximum amount of validated learning about customers with the least effort

- Network Effects: The network effect is a business principle that illustrates the idea that when more people use a product or service, its value increases. The network effect significantly applies to digital platforms, dating all the way back to the internet itself

- OKR (Objectives and Key Results): a goal-setting framework used by individuals, teams, and organisations to define measurable goals and track their outcomes

- Product Backlog; An ordered list of requirements of a product/solution, it is single source of work undertaken by the Development Team

- Product Owner/Manager: The product owner focuses on product goals—they're primarily concerned with bringing the product manager's vision to life by guiding the development team on what to do next and how. The product manager is responsible for the entire product management process, bringing the business closer to its goals. Both are critical roles but for smaller products, a separate product manager role may not be needed

- Retrospective: A meeting that is held at the end of each iteration for the team to reflect on how to become more effective, by inspecting the process, product, tools, people and interactions

- Scrum Master: A scrum master is a coach and a guide who ensures their team understands the scrum framework and its principles, values, and practices. They are a servant leader who helps their team in many ways

- Servant Leadership: Servant Leadership is a non-traditional leadership philosophy, embedded in a set of behaviours and practices that place the primary emphasis on the well-being of those being served.

- Self Organised Team: A self-organising team is one that does not depend on or wait for a manager to assign work. Instead, these teams find their own work and manage the associated responsibilities and timelines

- Sprint: A fixed length event of one month or less to create consistency. All work required to deliver an increment is done within sprints

- Taylorism: A factory management system developed in the late 19th century to increase efficiency by evaluating every step in a manufacturing process and breaking down production into specialised repetitive tasks so that workers could become effectively replaceable parts of the system

- User Story: An informal, general explanation of a software feature written from the perspective of the end user or customer

- Value Management Office: an organisational function responsible for facilitating Portfolio Management process, financial governance and operational excellence as part of a Lean-Agile transformation

- Value Stream: A representation of the series of steps that an organisation uses to implement Solutions that provide a continuous flow of value to a customer

- Velocity: An indication of the average amount of Product Backlog turned into an Increment of product during a Sprint by a Scrum Team, tracked by team for internal use and not inter-team comparison as it is based on relative estimations

- Vision: A vision statement identifies where the organisation wants or intends to be in future or where it should be to best meet the needs of the stakeholders

BIBLIOGRAPHY

1. https://www.gallup.com>indicator-employee-engagement
2. VUCA is an acronym to describe volatility, uncertainty, complexity and ambiguity of general conditions and situations. Bennis, Warren; Nanus, Burt (1985). Leaders: Strategies for Taking Charge.
3. J.Immelt - Restoring Trust, Speech, New York Economic Club, November4, 2002
4. Frederick Winslow Taylor was an American mechanical engineer. He was widely known for his methods to improve industrial efficiency. Production, he contended, was governed by universal and natural laws that were independent of human judgement. The object of scientific management was to discover these laws and apply the "one best way" to basic managerial functions such as selection, promotion, compensation, training, and production - Yonotan Reshef: Taylor's Scientific Management
5. Dr. Winston Royce, credited as being the creator of the 'Waterfall' in his seminal paper "Managing The Development of Large Software Systems" never mentions the word "waterfall". The knowledge work world has coined this term. And for good reason. Just like water can't go upwards in a waterfall, the sequential nature of the traditional PM process makes it extremely hard (and costly) for past "phases" to be repeated.
6. Collaboration Overload is Sinking Productivity - by Rob Cross, Mike Benson, Jack Kostal, and RJ Milnor, Harvard Business Review, Sep 7, 2021
7. Dr. Russel Ackoff : "A system is never the sum of its parts". It's the product of the interaction of its parts"
8. Rigby, Darrell K., Jeff Sutherland, and Hirotaka Takeuchi. "Embracing Agile: How to Master the Process That's Transforming Management." Harvard Business Review 94, no. 5 (May 2016)

9. It is mathematically proven and empirically experienced widely that when resource utilisation approaches high levels, waiting time and hence lead times disproportionately increase. This is obviously quite un-agile and hence a balance just be struck. This is especially true when there is variability which is quite common. Mathematically this has been expressed by many including the Kingman's equation.

10. Which Two Heads Are Better Than One, Juliet Bourke, Australian Institute of Company Directors, 2021

11. Mindset:The New Psychology of Success - Carol S. Dweck, Ballantine Books; 2007

12. A Transformation MVP (can also be called Minimum Viable Transformation or MVT) is an agreed set of minimum changes that is still comprehensive enough to result in a significant benefit for the organisation and/or its customers. It is a readily adaptable and lightweight chunk of a larger overall transformation - be it a total business transformation, or a digital transformation, a functional transformation or any other type. It prevents boiling the ocean and also generates quicker ROI for change. It also leads to lessons learned and course corrections if needed. One or more pilots may be included in a Transformation MVP or MVT and an iterative 'test and learn' element is built into the design of an MVT.

13. A Transformation Sprint, according to its developers Haydn Shaughnessy and Fin Goulding who came up with the term, is a 6-step process implemented within a timeboxed 4 weeks Sprint period. It is a templated approach that takes into account typical transformation related problems and offers a quick way to get from A to B.

14. Bezos recognised communicated as a matter of principle and practice in Amazon that waiting for 90% information for making a decision is too slow. Instead, Bezos encouraged making decisions with only 60% of the information so that windows of opportunity do not get missed.

15. Actually, Peter Drucker never said this, it is one of the most enduring and catchy misquotations.

16. 'From Shopping To Space Travel, How The Mainframe Changed Our World', Pat Toole, April8, 2014, Forbes

17. First Let's Fire All The Managers, December 201,Harvard Business Review, Gary Hamel

18. 'Accelerate' John P. Kotter, Harvard Business Review, Nov 2012

19. Successfully Transitioning To New Leadership Roles, Scott Keller, McKinsey Quarterly, May 2018

20. Shopify's CFO explains how its new meeting cost calculator works, and how it will cut 474,000 events in 2023: 'Time is Money' - Fortune, July 14,2023

21. The Cost Of Unnecessary Meeting Attendance, https://20067454.fs1.hubspotusercontent-na1.net/hubfs/20067454/Report_The%20Cost%20of%20Unnecessary%20Meeting%20Attendance.pdf

22. Lean Thinking' (1996) - James P Womack and Daniel T Jones

23. The Business Case For AI, Kavita Ganesan, Opinosis Analytics Publishing, 2022.

24. "Lean Accounting:Best Practices for Sustainable Integration" by Joe Stenzel, Catherine Stenzel, and Reza M. Pirasteh.

25. As per the story in Aesop's Fables, a farmer owns a goose that lays a golden egg every day. Instead of being patient, the farmer gets greedy and decides to cut open the goose, hoping to find all the golden eggs at once. However, he finds nothing, and the source of his wealth is lost. The fable teaches the lesson of not being too greedy and valuing long-term gains over short-term desires.

26. Tuckman, Bruce W (1965). "Developmental sequence in small groups". Psychological Bulletin.

27. The Innovator's Dilemma - The innovator's dilemma: Christensen, C. M. (1997) When new technologies cause great firms to fail. Harvard Business School Press.

28. Thomas J. Allen, Managing the Flow of Technology (Cambridge, MA: MIT Press).

29. Weinberg, Gerald M, Quality Software Management – Volume 1: Systems Thinking